School Improvement

What's in it for schools?

This book aims to de-mystify the principles and practice of school improvement by demonstrating how successful classroom and school improvement occurs. It outlines the conditions, strategies and approaches that promote sustainable improvement and provides an overview of the main theoretical perspectives in this area. This accessible text will be useful for practitioners working within schools and with schools, offering clear guidance for those keen to raise standards and improve achievement.

Alma Harris is Professor of School Leadership at the Institute of Education, University of Warwick. She is also a Research Associate of the International Centre for School Effectiveness and School Improvement at the Institute of Education, University of London.

What's in it for schools?

Edited by Kate Myers and John MacBeath

Inspection: What's in it for schools?

James Learmonth

Leadership: What's in it for schools?

Thomas J. Sergiovanni

Self-evaluation: What's in it for schools?

John MacBeath and Archie McGlynn

School Improvement: What's in it for schools?

Alma Harris

Page 7 ofsted and consequences

Page 11 leadership

P 12,13 Collegiate.

P.'5 . Formal.

School Improvement

What's in it for schools?

Alma Harris

RoutledgeFalmer
Taylor & Francis Group

LONDON AND NEW YORK

First published 2002
by RoutledgeFalmer
11 New Fetter Lane, London EC4P 4EE

Simultaneously published in the USA and Canada
by RoutledgeFalmer
29 West 35th Street, New York, NY 10001

Reprinted 2003

RoutledgeFalmer is an imprint of the Taylor & Francis Group

© 2002 Alma Harris

Typeset in Baskerville by
Keystroke, Jacaranda Lodge, Wolverhampton
Printed and bound in Great Britain by
TJ International Ltd, Padstow, Cornwall

British Library Cataloguing in Publication Data
A catalogue record for this book is available from the British Library

Library of Congress Cataloging in Publication Data
A catalog record for this book has been requested.

ISBN 0–415–24920–1 (hbk)
ISBN 0–415–24921–X (pbk)

To Christopher, Rhys, Gareth and Jaime,
their parents and teachers.

The true wealth of any society is simply its people. The real wealth
creators, are parents and teachers. Long term, everything else
depends on them.

Cardinal Hume

Contents

Tables

Series Editors' preface

Kate Myers and John MacBeath

Series introduction

There is a concerted move to raise standards in the public education system. The aim is laudable. Few people would disagree with it. However, there is no clear agreement about what we mean by 'standards'. Do we mean attainment or achievement more broadly defined, for example, and how we are to raise whatever it is we agree needs raising?

At the same time, there appears to be an increasing trend towards approaching changes in education through a controlling, rational and technical framework. This framework tends to concentrate on educational content and delivery and ignores the human resource perspective and the complexity of how human beings live, work and interact with one another. It overemphasises linearity and pays insufficient attention to how people respond to change and either support or subvert it.

Recent government initiatives, including the National Curriculum, OFSTED school and LEA inspections, assessment procedures, league tables, target-setting, literacy and numeracy hours, and performance management have endorsed this framework. On occasions this has been less to do with the content of 'reforms' than the process of implementation – that is, doing it 'to' rather than 'with' the teaching profession. Teachers are frequently treated as the problem rather than part of the solution, with the consequence that many feel disillusioned, demoralised and disempowered. Critics of this *top-down* approach are often seen as lacking rigour, complacent about standards, and uninterested in raising achievement.

We wanted to edit this series because we believe that you can be passionate about public education, about raising achievement, about ensuring that all pupils are entitled to the best possible education that society is able to provide – whatever their race, sex or class. We also believe that achieving this is not a simple matter of common sense or of the appliance of science – it is more complex than that. Most of all, we see the teaching profession as an important part of the solution to finding ways through these complexities.

What's in it for schools? is a series that will make educational policy issues relevant to practitioners. Each book in the series focuses on a major educational issue and raises key questions, such as:

- can inspection be beneficial to schools?
- how can assessment procedures help pupils learn?
- how can school self-evaluation improve teaching and learning?
- what impact does leadership in the school have in the classroom?
- how can school improvement become classroom improvement?

The books are grounded in sound theory, recent research evidence and best practice, and aim to:

- help you to make meaning personally and professionally from knowledge in a given field;
- help you to seek out practical applications of an area of knowledge for classrooms and schools;
- help those of you who want to research the field in greater depth, by providing key sources with accessible summaries and recommendations.

In addition, each chapter ends with a series of questions for reflection or further discussion, enabling schools to use the books as a resource for whole-school staff development.

We hope that the books in this series will show you that there are ways of raising achievement that can take account of how schools grow and develop and how teachers work and interact with one another. *What's in it for schools?* – a great deal, we think!

Acknowledgements

In writing a book on school improvement it is inevitable that the work of those in the field is included and represented. I am fortunate to be part of a research community that is intellectually supportive, generous and challenging. This book recognises those within the school-effectiveness and school improvement research fields who have contributed so much to schools and continue to work relentlessly on their behalf.

Warm and sincere thanks go to those researchers and writers who have inspired and helped me over the years. Their support and friendship means a great deal and while it would be impossible to name them all there are those who deserve my special thanks. I'm particularly grateful for the warmth, generosity and academic stewardship of David Hopkins, Peter Mortimore, Louise Stoll, Pam Sammons, Andy Hargreaves, Lorna Earl, Jon Young, Ben Levin, Kate Myers, John MacBeath, Judith Warren Little, Lesley Saunders, Karen Seashore Louis and Bill Mulford. Much of their work is reflected in these pages.

Also, thanks must go to all the LEA advisers, headteachers and teachers I have worked with and continue to work with across many countries. Their commitment to and belief in school improvement makes all the difference.

Introduction

The growth of interest in school improvement has been striking. In less than a decade, school improvement has become an expectation of all schools across many Western countries. In the UK, as in many other educational systems, school improvement has become a dominant theme in contemporary educational reform and development. The growing concern amongst politicians and the wider public about 'educational standards' has resulted in a wide variety of school improvement interventions and initiatives. Some of these have been government directed while others have been locally initiated and developed. Yet, despite a wide variety of activities in the name of school improvement, there is still a tendency for schools to focus change efforts at the whole-school level rather than at the level of the classroom. Many schools have equated improvement with restructuring and have operated a model of school improvement predicated upon changing the management arrangements or systems within the school (Hopkins *et al.*, 1997).

It has become increasingly apparent that restructuring or re-organising rarely impacts upon student achievement and learning (Fullan, 1991: 2). While it cannot be denied that there are conditions at the school level which can make classroom improvement more possible, the teaching and learning process remains the main determinant of educational outcomes (Creemers, 1994). The school improvement research base highlights the centrality of teaching and learning in the pursuit of sustained school improvement. It reiterates the importance of multi-level intervention and of mobilising change at school, department and classroom level (Fullan, 1992; Hopkins *et al.*, 1994; Hopkins and Harris, 1997).

Successful school improvement is dependent upon the school's ability to manage change and development. As Hopkins (2001: 2) suggests, 'real' improvement 'is best regarded as a strategy for educational change that focuses on student achievement by modifying classroom practice and adapting the management arrangements within the school to support teaching and learning'. This necessitates building the 'capacity' for change and development within the school as an organisation. Capacity-building is concerned with creating the conditions, opportunities and experiences for development and mutual learning. Building the capacity for school improvement necessitates paying careful attention to how collaborative processes in schools are fostered and developed. It implies that 'individuals feel confident in their own capacity, in the capacity of their colleagues and in the capacity of the school to promote professional development' (Mitchell and Sackney 2000: 78). But how do schools create the capacity for change? What are the strategies that result in effective change and development at school and classroom level?

It has been suggested that 'guides to school improvement have a conceptual hole at their centre. They never seem to offer help in answering three key questions, what will you do to improve? How? And why?' (Ouston, 1999: 173). This book attempts to address the question of 'how to improve' by outlining the principles and describing the process of school improvement. It looks at how schools generate the external capacity and build the internal capability for improvement. It outlines the conditions, strategies and approaches that promote sustainable and continuous improvement. The book provides an overview of the main theoretical perspectives on classroom and school improvement and draws upon the extensive school improvement research base. Its central aim is to illustrate *how* successful school and classroom improvement occurs. This book is a summary and a synthesis of the key elements of the process of school improvement. Consequently, it is primarily intended for those working both within schools and with schools.

The book inevitably draws upon the extensive school improvement literature in order to address the question of *how schools improve*. It does not claim to be the definitive text in the school improvement field but rather an overview and a synthesis of what works. Throughout the book the work of leading researchers and writers in the field is acknowledged. Without their significant and substantial contribution, there would be little to say about how schools improve and sustain improvement over time. In particular this book owes a great deal to the work of David Hopkins and to colleagues who are part of the 'Improving the Quality of Education for All' project.[1] The ideas that inform and shape the work of this highly successful school improvement project are reflected throughout the chapters.

Structure

The book consists of eight chapters and the structure of the book is as follows. Chapter 1 introduces the concept of school improvement and outlines the current context for school development and change. It focuses particularly upon the standards-based accountability policies that have impacted upon schools in the last decade. Against this backdrop, the chapter explores the dimensions of successful school improvement and outlines the prerequisites of effective school development and change. Chapter 2 considers effective school improvement and looks at school improvement projects that have resulted in improved teaching and learning. In particular, the chapter explores how effective school improvement is achieved. It focuses upon the ways in which improvements in teaching and learning are secured and how the conditions for classroom improvement are generated.

Chapter 3 considers the complex but essential relationship between change and school improvement. The chapter describes the process of change and outlines how change is best promoted and sustained within schools. It also considers how school-based evaluation can assist and inform the change process. Chapter 4 explores how schools build the capacity and capability for change. It focuses upon the roles and responsibilities of 'change agents' in supporting schools through the process of change and development.

Chapter 5 considers the relationship between leadership and school improvement. It compares different leadership approaches and highlights how leadership at different levels within the school is a necessary part of building the capacity for change. In particular, it suggests that teacher leadership is an important contributor to successful school and

1 'Improving the Quality of Education for All', IQEA is one of the most successful improvement projects in the UK.

classroom change. Chapter 6 looks at issues of improving classrooms through promoting effective teaching and learning. It considers how professional development contributes to school improvement and looks at ways in which teachers can promote effective learning within the classroom.

Chapter 7 looks at the processes associated with teachers' professional development and the ways in which professional learning can be enhanced and developed. Chapter 8 considers the future directions for school improvement and discusses a variety of ways in which schools can work together to build the capacity for school improvement.

It is hoped that those working in schools will use the ideas presented in the book as a reference point or a guide to their own improvement efforts. Successful school improvement can only occur when schools apply those strategies that best fit their own context and particular developmental needs. Consequently, a first step in the process of school improvement is to diagnose and identify the developmental needs that exist within the school and subsequently to select the most appropriate improvement strategies.

As schools face continuous pressure to raise standards and to improve performance there will be increased demand for school improvement strategies that work. This book provides some of the ways in which improvement can be fostered and developed, there are others. Most importantly, the model of school improvement presented in this book is one that acknowledges the differences between schools and reinforces that improvement is a process that individual schools need to embrace for their own developmental purposes.

Unfortunately, there is no universal panacea or 'blueprint' for successful school improvement. As Hopkins (2001: 2) warns, 'the emergence of school improvement from the shadows is a mixed blessing. As with any new idea, much is expected of it, particularly from those desperately seeking simple and rapid solutions to complex challenges. School improvement's time in the sun will be short lived unless it can persuade its new found friends that it is not a quick-fix response to educational change.' There are, however, some helpful signposts and levers that schools can use to generate their *own* improvement capacity and capability. This book highlights various approaches to improvement and suggests some strategies that schools might use. The most successful school improvement projects across many countries reinforce the message that for school improvement to work most effectively improvement cannot be a 'bolt on' activity. They recognise that school improvement is not a single activity or approach but a powerful set of processes that can significantly enhance the quality of teaching and learning. School improvement is not a fad or a fashion but a systematic way of generating change and development within the school.

The success of any school improvement effort will ultimately depend on the context in which it takes place. It will not occur by chance but requires a conscious effort to create an environment that is supportive of risk-taking and mutual learning. Explicit efforts need to be made to foster trust, to develop the relationships within the school and to create the conditions for improvement to occur. School leaders have an important role to play in creating these conditions but ultimately, school improvement is a collective endeavour that is fundamentally concerned with building a professional learning community where teachers and students develop and learn together.

1 School improvement in context

Introduction

Over the past thirty years the school improvement research field has become a powerful influence in both educational policy and practice. The message that *schools make a difference* has provided the rationale for various school improvement programmes and reform efforts. These have varied in scope and scale but all have been focused upon increasing student performance and achievement. One common way in which governments across many countries have sought to improve schools is through restructuring the education system. Within the United States, in particular, school restructuring has been a central component of educational reform and has dominated school improvement efforts. Yet, the success of restructuring as a means of improving schools remains questionable.

As Fullan (1999: 1) notes, 'we have been innovating for student improvement for most of this century yet the extent to which this has resulted in improvement in the life chances of students is debatable'. The concentration on system-level reform and change has propagated a view of school improvement that is 'top-down', that is concerned with outcomes rather than processes. The preoccupation with 'outcome-led' school improvement has resulted in a drive for greater accountability and system-wide reform that is premised upon improvement in standards and performance.

Across many countries there has been a substantial shift towards greater central control over education systems and a 'standards-driven' agenda for reform in schools. In England and Wales, in particular, there has been increasing central government control over core aspects of the educational process. The implementation of the National Curriculum under the Education Reform Act (1988) heralded the start of greater government control over schools and schooling. The subsequent introduction of national testing, OFSTED inspection and performance management has further reinforced an accountability-driven and centrally controlled education system.

Under this system schools are held accountable for their performance and 'failure' has serious penalties and consequences. Most recently, it has been announced that schools who are deemed to be failing will be in receipt of a tougher process of inspection. They will be called to account and tough sanctions will be enforced if they are unable to raise performance. Interestingly, those schools that find themselves in the most difficult socio-economic contexts will be placed under even greater pressure to improve.

There is a growing recognition that simply applying more pressure upon schools to improve is unlikely to yield positive results. Within the research and practitioner communities it is clear that there are no easy solutions or *quick fixes* to the challenge of improving school performance (Stoll and Myers, 1998). While the OFSTED inspection process offers a mechanism for diagnosing the areas for development and change, the extent to which it leads to long-term school or classroom improvement remains debatable (Chapman, 2000). It is clear that schools require strategies for improvement that match their particular context, circumstances and developmental need. The 'one size fits all approach' to school improvement fundamentally misunderstands the process of school and classroom-level change (Stoll and Myers, 1998).

Yet the goal of trying to find feasible ways to raise standards and improve classrooms has become a central preoccupation with policy-makers. Although the nature of reform varies due to the unique combinations of historical, cultural, institutional and political factors, there have been a number of common elements of reform across a number of countries. Hopkins and Levin (2000: 18–19) suggest that in the larger scheme reforms have tended to focus on:

- *Curriculum*: governments have instituted more restrictive curriculum requirements including increased emphasis on science, technology, and basic skills such as literacy.

- *Accountability*: governments have increased testing of students and have made the results public, and in some cases put in place extensive external inspection of schools.
- *Governance*: while governments have centralised curriculum and assessment, they have also decentralised many decisions from intermediate bodies such as local authorities to individual schools, and have given parents an increased role in school governance, all of which has put new pressures on professional staff.
- *Market forces*: governments have tried to introduce market elements to schooling through increasing the opportunity – or requirement – for parents to choose schools (or, in some cases, for schools to choose parents and students).
- *Status of teachers*: in a number of countries the status of teachers and their organisations has been attacked directly through unilateral changes by governments to the status of unions or to collective bargaining arrangements.

One prevalent strategy, across many countries, has been to centralise educational control whilst at the same time decentralising the responsibility for implementation. In the UK, the question of how to improve student achievement has resulted in the adoption of an ambitious reform programme aimed at raising standards in schools. National literacy and numeracy strategies have been introduced, ICT in the curriculum has been stressed and a major initiative designed to improve teaching and learning at Key Stage 3 is underway. In addition, the problem of underachievement is being addressed on several different fronts through:

- the regulation of the curriculum;
- inspection of the quality of management and teaching in the school;
- tighter control and direction of initial teacher training;
- sanctions and imposed targets for improvement.

The message constantly being reinforced is that all schools, irrespective of their social and economic situation, can succeed and improve. Yet there is evidence to suggest that in the most challenging circumstances schools face a range of problems that prevent significant gains in improvements being made. The social limits of school reform are all too evident and are highlighted by Thrupp (1999: 182), who notes: 'We should bear in mind that being optimistic about school reform has helped avoid dealing with tough questions about the impact on education of social inequalities of power and resources.' Thrupp also suggests that the politics of polarisation and blame that are prevalent in many education systems serve to widen social class disparities.

> Schools which lose in educational markets are seen as those whose teachers and principals have not been able to improve enough to boost their own reputation and hence the size of student intake. The running down and eventual failure of such schools can therefore be justified by being simply the price paid for a quality education system.
>
> (Thrupp, 1999: 6)

Writers such as Slee *et al.* (1998) and Morley and Rassol (1999) have argued that those involved in school improvement have taken insufficient account of the socio-economic context in which schools find themselves. The 'marketisation' of education has exacerbated differences between schools in different socio-economic settings. Schools with little parental or community support face a particularly difficult school improvement task.

Differential school improvement strategies are required for schools in varying socio-economic contexts. Improvement approaches are needed that match the growth state of the school and fit its particular set of developmental needs. Hopkins (2001: 3) suggests:

> Put simply, schools at different stages of development require different strategies not only to enhance their capacity for development, but also to provide a more effective education for their students. Strategies for school development need to fit the 'growth state' or culture of the particular school. Strategies which are effective for improving performance at one growth state are not necessarily effective at another.

This implies that schools will need to be highly discerning in selecting school improvement strategies and approaches. In a postmodern society where all schools will be faced with increased waves of uncertainty and unpredictability even more caution is needed in approaching development and change. The legacy of 'innovation overload' is well known and where schools face multiple changes and competing priorities improvement is unlikely to occur. Fullan (1999: 4) suggests schools will need to cope with the powerful and competing forces of stability and change. He argues that 'success lies in sustaining an organisation in the borders between stability and instability. This is a state of chaos, a difficult to maintain dissipative structure.' Therefore, schools facing uncertain or changing conditions need to invest in their own learning and to embrace those improvement strategies that best meet the needs of their students and their teachers.

School improvement

There are many definitions of school improvement and various interpretations of school improvement as a process. Miles *et al.* (1987: 3) define school improvement 'as a systematic, sustained effort aimed at change in learning conditions and other related internal conditions in one or more schools with the ultimate aim of accomplishing educational goals more effectively'. Hopkins (1996: 32) suggests that there are two senses in which the term school improvement is generally used. The first, 'is a common sense meaning which relates to general efforts to make schools better places for students and [for] students to learn'. The second is a more technical or specific definition in which Hopkins (1996: 32) defines school improvement as a 'strategy for educational change that enhances student outcomes as well as strengthening the school's capacity for managing change'.

This definition highlights the importance of school improvement as a process of changing school culture. It views the school as the centre of change and teachers as an intrinsic part of the change process. It suggests that for school improvement to occur teachers need to be committed to the process of change which will involve them in examining and changing their own practice. This definition is used throughout the book to encompass those approaches and strategies collectively known as school improvement and which focus upon changing school culture rather than structure.

Barth (1990: 45) reinforces a view of school improvement that embraces cultural change. 'What needs to be improved about schools is their culture, the quality of inter-personal relationships, and the nature and quality of learning experiences'. Some underlying assumptions about school improvement therefore are as follows:

- Schools have the capacity to improve themselves, if the conditions are right. A major responsibility of those inside the school is to help provide these conditions for those outside.
- School improvement is an effort to determine and provide, from without and within, conditions under which the adults and youngsters who inhabit schools will promote and sustain learning among themselves (Barth, 1990: 45).

These assumptions emphasise that school improvement is largely concerned with changing the internal practices of schools by influencing how people work together. Implicit within this interpretation is a belief that school culture can be changed and that cultural change is achieved through changing the internal conditions within the school.

Research findings across many countries have contributed to a comprehensive model of educational change. This shows how change is initiated, implemented and institutionalised (Fullan, 1991). The model has highlighted a number of important findings about the process of successful school change. Firstly, school improvement research has demonstrated the vital importance of *teacher development* in school-level change. It has consistently shown that teacher development in inextricably linked to school development and is an essential part of school improvement (Hopkins *et al.*, 1994). Secondly, school improvement research has reinforced the importance of *leadership* in securing school-level change. It has shown that leaders within improving schools have vision and drive change forward. It has also demonstrated that within improving schools leadership is shared and distributed (Harris *et al.*, 2001).

Thirdly, school improvement work has shown that there is *no one blueprint for action* but approaches to improvement will vary across different types of school. It has directly challenged the assumption of the *one-size-fits-all* approach to improvement by demonstrating the importance of matching improvement strategy to school type (Hopkins *et al.*, 2000). Fourthly, the school improvement movement has reinforced the necessity of relating change efforts to specific student outcomes. It has emphasised the importance of focusing attention at the *student level* and of improving teaching and learning conditions within the classroom (Hopkins *et al.* 1997). Finally, the school improvement movement has demonstrated the importance of understanding and working with *school culture*. The field has consistently shown that a school culture that promotes collegiality, trust and collaborative working relationships and that focuses upon teaching and learning is more likely to be self-renewing and responsive to improvement efforts (Hopkins, 2000).

REFLECTION

Think about your own school:
1   How would you define improvement within your own school context?
2   What evidence would you need to collect to demonstrate that school improvement was taking place?
3   Who are the key players in securing school improvement?
4   What are the challenges facing your school in terms of improvement?

School culture

Within the school improvement literature, the school is viewed as an organic and dynamic culture. A key assumption within the literature is that improvement strategies can result in changing school culture and that leadership has an important part to play in defining and shaping culture. School improvement researchers have tended to emphasise certain norms and values that shape individual and collective activity at the school level. The types of school cultures that tend to support improvement are those that are collaborative, have collegiate working relationships and have a climate for change.

Establishing a positive climate for change is an important pre-requisite for school improvement. This climate should facilitate learning within the organisation and support those engaged in the learning. Building a positive climate involves:

- establishing trust amongst colleagues;
- inviting them to participate;
- affirming their ideas;
- providing opportunities for innovation and risk-taking.

Within an improving school trust is an important component. Walker *et al.* (1998: 2) suggest that trust is a necessary element for building a learning community:

> As people work together to sustain healthy practice and build new ways of learning and relating to one another, it does not take long for the subject of trust or trustworthiness to enter the conversation. At the very least, the importance and pervasiveness of trust are implicit in our very effort to establish communities of learners and the generative setting for the expression of our shared educational ambitions.

According to these writers trust is a required element for generating school improvement. It is the social glue that links a learning community and allows teachers to work collaboratively. In schools teachers need to trust their colleagues and senior management, otherwise cultural change is unlikely to occur. Research implies that trust is particularly important when the risks are high or when large-scale change is imminent. As Mitchell and Sackney (2000: 49) note:

> trust is a critical factor in bringing about profound improvement to a school. Without trust, people divert their energy into self-protection and away from learning. Where trust is lacking, people will not take the risks necessary to move the school forward. When distrust pervades a school culture, it is unlikely that the school will be an energetic, motivating place. Instead a culture of self-preservation and isolation is likely to pervade the school.

Writers in the field emphasise the importance of collaborative cultures for school development and growth. The centrality of collegiality and trust in pursuit of school improvement is undisputed but there are many schools where the culture is far from collegial. Myers (1995) talks about the pathology of schools and has highlighted how certain types of culture can negatively affect development and performance. Research has shown that ineffective schools have particular cultures that are characterised by dysfunctional staff relationships and insufficient focus on teaching and learning. They tend to be cultures where dissonant values emerge rendering the culture fragmented. Work by Rosenholtz (1989), Hopkins (2001) and Stoll and Fink (1996) has demonstrated how different types of school culture can affect the possibility and practicality of school-level change. This work has also shown how negative socio-cultural conditions can actively prevent improvement.

It is clear that dysfunctional school cultures are difficult to permeate and can undermine school improvement activity. Deal and Peterson's (1994) work on balancing logic and artistry in schools considers the impact of negative school cultures. They suggest that one way of dealing with a dysfunctional culture is to give people a chance to vent their feelings and to discuss the culture in which they work. Another way is to encourage staff within the school to diagnose their school culture by comparing and contrasting it to a cultural typology. Hargreaves (1994: 16) has proposed four 'ideal types' of school culture:

*   *the formal school culture* characterised by pressure on students to achieve learning goals but weak social cohesion between staff and students;
*   *a welfarist culture* where relations between staff and students are relaxed and friendly but there is little academic pressure;
*   *a hothouse culture* which pressurises staff and students to participate in all aspects of school life, academic and social;
*   *a survivalist culture* characterised by poor social relations and low academic achievement.

Hargreaves (1994) argues that the ideal culture for an improving school is one which balances academic pressure and social cohesion:

> Expectations of work and conduct are high – the principal's expectations of staff and the teachers' of students. Yet these standards are not perceived to be unreasonable; everyone is supported in striving for them and rewarded for reaching them. For both teachers and students, school is a demanding but very enjoyable place to be.
>
> (1994: 11)

In order to commence the process of school improvement, it is initially necessary to *diagnose* the particular culture of the school.

REFLECTION

- What is the dominant culture of your school?
- How well do staff work together?
- How could your school culture be changed for the better?
- What needs to happen to change your school culture?

Improving schools tend to hold a balance between what Hopkins *et al.* (1996: 23) describe as maintenance and developmental activities. Their maintenance activities are the routine or 'everyday' activities needed to keep the school operating. They are the everyday administrative tasks and system activities. The developmental activities are those that are necessary to move the school forward. They help ensure the growth of the school. Using these two dimensions and drawing upon the work of Hopkins (2001) and Stoll and Fink (1996), it is possible to identify different types of schools: improving, failing, trapped and dynamic.

Improving schools

Studies of improving schools have shown that they tend to be well organised with efficient systems for recording and reviewing progress. They place a high emphasis on maintenance and are good on the day-to-day routine management tasks and requirements. In addition, these schools are actively involved in their own development but select areas for development and change very carefully. They provide opportunities for staff to work together but create a balance between maintenance and development. They are schools where there is a continual drive for improvement and where teachers are involved in change and development.

The failing school

At the other end of the spectrum is the visibly failing school which is low on development and low on maintenance. These schools are poor at the day-to-day management tasks and tend to be reactive rather than proactive in their approach to deadlines or problem solving. The lack of leadership in such schools means that the necessary organisation and planning is not in place. In addition, the culture of fragmentation evident in these schools means that development is not possible as the fundamental infrastructure necessary to support such development is not in place. These failing schools are not collegiate and do not have clearly articulated goals, plans and vision.

The trapped school

Trapped schools are those that undertake all the necessary maintenance activities but neglect developmental work. These schools are not obviously failing as they appear to be efficiently run. However, their reluctance to develop or to take on new ideas means that they will, at best, remain where they are and, at worst, gradually deteriorate. Without an investment in their development such schools will be unlikely to improve. They have the potential to make an enormous contribution to student performance and achievement but need to unlock this potential by investing in development and change.

The dynamic school

Dynamic schools tend to approach innovation with great enthusiasm and are viewed by those outside the school in a highly positive way. These schools tend to be viewed by the external world as lively and exciting. These schools like to see themselves as 'go ahead' and dynamic but often drive forward innovation at the expense of maintenance activities. On the surface such schools might be mistaken as moving because of their high level of involvement in change and innovation. But the opportunity cost of high levels of development is the neglect of basic maintenance activities. Dynamic schools can also be places where fragmentation operates underneath the surface and where innovation overload is a real possibility.

While the diagnosis of school culture is an important first step on the road to school improvement, the next step must be changing school culture for the better. In those schools that are visibly failing, the requirements for cultural change may be obvious but will require sensitive intervention. For those schools falling into the 'dynamic' or 'trapped' categories the issue will be one of selecting strategies that match the developmental need of the school. For the improving school the task will be to ensure that the positive culture is nurtured and sustained. For all schools embarking upon school improvement the central issue is one of changing or reinforcing culture.

While there are no easy answers to school improvement there are some core activities that have been shown to lead to cultural change. Some of the behaviours used to strengthen the school culture include reinforcing with staff, norms of excellence for their own work, assisting staff to clarify shared beliefs and values and to act in accord with such beliefs and values. Leithwood *et al.* (1999: 39) propose that cultural change in schools involves a number of core activities:

- setting directions (includes vision building, goal consensus and the development of high performance expectations);
- developing people (includes the provision of individualized support, intellectual stimulation and the modelling of values and practices important to the mission of the school);
- organising (culture building in which colleagues are motivated by moral imperatives and structuring, fostering shared decision-making processes and problem solving capacities);
- building relationships with the school community.

These behaviours have been shown to encourage teacher collaboration, to increase teacher motivation and to improve teachers' self-efficacy. There is evidence to demonstrate a positive relationship between such approaches and school improvement. Culture-building includes behaviours aimed at developing school norms, values, beliefs and assumptions that are student-centred and support continuing professional development. Good leaders not only manage structure but they purposefully impact upon the culture in order to change it. In summary the goal of school improvement is to bring about positive *cultural change* by altering the processes that occur within the school. For long-term, sustained school improvement to occur there has to be deep-rooted change *inside* the school.

Inside school improvement

Successful school improvement efforts embody the core principle that change and development are owned by the school rather than imposed from outside (Hopkins *et al.*, 1996). School improvement rests on a number of key assumptions:

- schools have the capacity to improve themselves;
- school improvement involves cultural change;
- there are school level and classroom level conditions for change;
- school improvement is concerned with building greater capacity for change (Van Vezlen *et al.*, 1985; Hopkins, 1987 and 1990).

Successful school improvement involves building capacity for change at both the school and the classroom level (Ainscow *et al.*, 1994; Fullan, 1991; Harris, 2000c). Interventions in teaching and learning are essential but on their own will not result in sustainable improvements in levels of achievement. The crucial point is that in terms 'of school development, neither external nor internal strategies will impact upon the progress of students unless the strategy itself impacts at the same time on the internal conditions or change capacity of the school or schools' (Hopkins *et al.*, 1996: 36).

Creating sustainable conditions means first understanding the culture that exists in the school and second deciding upon the norms and values that need to be changed. The kind of learning community that fosters school improvement implies a deep change in the views of professional practice, of people and of school organisations. Hopkins *et al.* (1994) define school improvement 'as strengthening the school's capacity for managing change'. Within the process of school improvement, no one can tell people what to do. They have to be allowed to search for their own solutions and to instigate and manage change inside their own institutions.

There are a number of important factors that contribute to change and improvement within a school:

1   *Participation*: any change requires teachers to participate in planning and decision-making.
2   *Commitment*: teachers need to be committed to the change as they will be instrumental in implementing it.
3   *Pressure and support*: change requires the pressure for change to occur and the technical/emotional support to ensure that change happens.
4   *External agency*: assistance from external sources such as consultants or LEA advisors is an important dimension of the change process. The provision of external agency can prevent innovation from being blocked and can ensure that the momentum for change is maintained.
5   *Staff development*: staff development activities need to be put in place to provide ongoing support for the new programme. The staff-development activities have to be task-specific and geared to teachers' concerns and skills.

There are also certain factors that will prevent school improvement from occurring:

1   Unclear purposes and goals: if the reasons for the change are not transparent it is unlikely that teachers will be committed to working towards the change.
2   Competing priorities: when there are many changes taking place simultaneously then the constraint of time will mean that some changes are given more priority than others.
3   Lack of support: in order to implement change there needs to be adequate technical, professional and emotional support for teachers.
4   Insufficient attention to implementation: many school improvement efforts fail simply because insufficient thought has been given to exactly *how* change is to be embedded within schools and classrooms. Fullan (1999) refers to this as the 'implementation dip' where all well-intentioned change is lost.
5   Inadequate leadership: any successful change or innovation will require direction and leadership. Where school improvement 'fails' it is often because it has lacked leadership within the school or has been delegated to others without the authority to take it forward.

Whether school improvement succeeds or fails will depend upon the way in which it is internally led and managed. However, there is no single optimum way to embark upon school improvement. Each school will have its own agenda, participants, resources and priorities. Each school is an enormously complicated social organism – there can be no crisp set of remedies, no unequivocal answers – the school does not readily lend itself to improvement on the basis of such generalisations.

Certain writers have commented upon the school as a 'ecosystem' as a way of trying to explain complex relationships.

> I believe we are moving towards a situation where schools operate in the ecological paradigm as places of choice, places of security . . . places where students and adults focus on things that matter to them and to their deepening understanding of the world.
>
> (Clarke, 2000: 21)

This view of schooling highlights the importance of seeing schools as complex, organic systems that are both responsive and reactive to change. It also challenges the traditional view of schools where control and power reside at the top of the organisation and where there is one best way to achieve certain outcomes. Taking an ecological perspective offers a different worldview where schools are living organisms that construct and define their own meanings. They are places that generate learning and build the capability to improve.

There are two fundamental questions that schools need to consider:

* How do we create and sustain school improvement?
* How do we ensure that school improvement impacts directly on student learning and achievement?

These two questions are interrelated and should be at the heart of any school improvement endeavour. The first refers to the processes and procedures that might be put in place to generate improvement at school and classroom level. The second relates to the impact of school improvement and how that impact is gauged. In considering school improvement, it is important to make a distinction between short-term and long-term approaches. A short-term response to school improvement will be one that is tactical, reactive and required to address a particular issue or problem. Alternatively, long-term approaches are much more strategic and proactive representing a holistic approach to school development and change. A long-term strategic approach will be directly related to the vision and core purposes of the school. It will also address the particular developmental needs of the individual school and ensure that the developmental priorities are met.

There are certain approaches, models and strategies that have been shown to be successful in mobilising school development, change and improvement. The next chapter compares school improvement programmes across a range of countries and distils those improvement strategies and approaches that have proved to be most effective.

QUESTIONS FOR FURTHER EXPLORATION

This chapter suggests that an important starting point on the road to school improvement is diagnosis of the school's developmental priorities. How far have the developmental priorities in your school resulted from a careful analysis of:

(a) strengths and weaknesses
(b) data
(c) school culture
(d) school context
(e) progress and performance?

School improvement is dependent upon an accurate diagnosis of developmental needs and the matching of appropriate school improvement strategies to meet those needs. How far is the current developmental work in your school:

(a) A result of careful analysis and diagnosis of need?

(b)   Coordinated and coherent?
(c)   Related to specific student learning outcomes?

What steps are needed to ensure that all developmental work within your school:

(a)   Is focused on real rather than perceived need?
(b)   Encompasses change at the classroom level?
(c)   Is evaluated to gauge impact?

2 Improving schools: what works?

Introduction

Although there are a large number of school improvement projects internationally, there remain relatively few that have been replicated successfully in a number of countries. School improvement projects that have been shown to be highly effective in one context are often difficult to implement in another. As Stoll *et al.* (2000: 1) note, 'solutions are sometimes transported from one country to another with little attention to the context in which the original solution originated or that of the receiving country'. There are some exceptions to this rule. For example, 'Success for All', 'Improving the Quality of Education for All' and the 'Coalition of Essential Schools' are improvement projects that are successfully operating in countries other than the UK (Slavin, 1996; Hopkins, 2000). However, in many cases, school improvement projects do not cross international boundaries, partly because of fundamental differences between educational systems but also because interpretations of concepts differ from country to country (Reynolds *et al.*, 1994).

Research currently underway is developing a common evaluative framework to compare and contrast case studies of effective school improvement within and across countries (Stoll *et al.*, 2000). The findings are providing important insights into some of the barriers that prevent the movement of school improvement projects across country boundaries. For example, the degree of centralisation and decentralisation across educational systems varies enormously, as do understandings of terms such as 'effectiveness' and 'improvement'. The European School Improvement Project has highlighted the many differences between countries and suggests that 'borrowing and applying successful initiatives from other countries without exploring the subtleties of those country contexts and how they interact may well prove a short sighted strategy' (Stoll *et al.*, 2000: 18). It also questions whether it is possible to develop a language of understanding about school improvement across diverse systems and contexts.

While the difficulties of in-depth comparisons of school improvement projects cannot be underestimated, the sheer volume of international improvement activity affords some examination of 'what works'. While projects may have different emphases, theoretical orientations and different approaches to school-level change it is possible to highlight some common components of effective school improvement. In order to chart the vast school improvement, Hopkins *et al.* (1994: 4) offer a useful categorisation that delineates between *organic* and *mechanistic* projects. School improvement work that is *organic* suggests broad principles, or general strategies within which schools are likely to flourish. Conversely, school improvement projects that are *mechanistic* provide direct guide-lines and are highly specific in the strategies they prescribe. This broad classification derived from Hopkins *et al.* (1994) provides a framework for mapping the school improvement projects that have been most influential in the field and that have been shown to work over time.

Successful school improvement: what works?

In many respects, the International School Improvement Project (ISIP) laid the cornerstone for subsequent school improvement programmes (Van Velzen *et al.*, 1985). Spanning four years from 1982 to 1986, this project, coordinated by the OECD, united fourteen countries and a wealth of expertise upon the subject of school improvement. The ISIP proposed a different way of thinking about school-level change which contrasted with the top-down approaches of the 1970s. Taking the school as the centre of change, the project embodied the long-term goal of moving schools towards the position of self-renewal and growth. This *organic* approach to school improvement highlighted the importance of taking a multi-level perspective on school development and change.

Other highly successful school improvement projects have been formed on the basis that they promote a particular philosophy. Some of these projects have taken the form of networks where schools subscribe to a shared set of principles. In essence, these projects provide a 'school improvement club' where admission is dependent upon agreeing to a set of project rules and guidelines. James Comer's School Development programme (Comer, 1988), the Coalition of Essential Schools (Sizer, 1989) and the League of Professional Schools at the University of Georgia led by Carl Glickman (1993) all fall into this category and have an increasing number of schools within their networks.

Another group of highly successful school improvement programmes have taken a less open-ended approach to school-level change. These programmes include the Halton Project (Stoll and Fink, 1996), the Accelerated Schools Project (1991), and certain approaches to restructuring in the USA (Elmore, 1995; Murphy and Louis, 1994). All these projects place the schools at the focal point of change and engage them in the process of school-growth planning. In addition, attention is also paid to the development of clear decision-making structures and building collaborative cultures within schools (Stoll and Fink, 1996).

'Improving the Quality of Education for All' (IQEA) similarly focuses upon building collaborative cultures in schools. As one of the most successful school improvement projects in the UK, IQEA is premised on the view that 'without an equal focus on the development capacity, or internal conditions of the school, innovative work quickly becomes marginalised' (Hopkins and Harris, 1997: 3). The project has developed a number of school and classroom conditions that support and sustain improvement (Ainscow *et al.*, 1994; Hopkins *et al.*, 1997). Each school within IQEA is encouraged to work upon the school-level and classroom-level conditions simultaneously (Harris and Hopkins, 1999).

Essentially IQEA is a model of school change that is premised upon facilitating cultural change within schools. It is not prescriptive in terms of what schools actually do, but does define the parameters for development. It provides an overarching model for school improvement which schools subsequently adapt for their own purposes and fit to their particular needs and context. IQEA is research driven and encourages schools not only to engage in their own internal enquiry but also to utilise the external research base concerning effective teaching and learning.

Other school improvement projects which are organic in nature are those that are based upon a partnership model with schools and the local education authority (LEA). The 'Schools Make a Difference' project in London (Myers, 1996) and the Lewisham School Improvement project characterise this type of approach. Both have specifically emphasised the role of the LEA in development and change. The impetus for change in these projects is locally owned, externally supported and school-initiated. In all of these projects external support, although often welcomed, is not entirely necessary throughout the project as the school searches out and creates its own support networks. Exposure to new ideas and practices, collaboration through consortia or 'pairing' arrangements are common in this type of school improvement work. Primarily, programmes of this type interface at the whole-school level but provide much-needed support and incentive for change at the classroom level.

At the other end of the school improvement spectrum are projects which fall into the *mechanistic* category in the respect that they advocate or prescribe a particular approach to school improvement. Early examples of such approaches include the self-managing approach to school improvement developed in the mid-1980s (Caldwell and Spinks, 1988). This approach has been widely disseminated and is based upon a management cycle that has six phases, i.e. goal-setting, policy-making, planning, preparation, implementation and evaluation. Although this cycle is now fairly commonplace, this 'step by step' approach has not proved successful with all schools. It is clear that this instrumental approach and others like it do not take into account the variability of schools and school context. Such *mechanistic* approaches presuppose uniformity both within the organisation and across organisations.

The High Reliability Schools project in the UK characterises a school improvement project designed to ensure that there are high levels of conformity between schools. This project is premised upon work by Stringfield (1995) which argues that educational systems have much to learn from the organisational processes of highly reliable organisations within the corporate and state-owned sectors. The characteristics of highly reliable organisations include effective training programmes, concentration on a few goals, standard operation procedures, attention to minor detail and identifying and rectifying weak links (Reynolds *et al.*, 1996). The research concerning High Reliability Schools (HRS) is ongoing but some evaluative evidence is available. The message from this work is that 'HRS principles and technology and the emphasis upon reliability are all generative of enhanced student outcomes but that optimum gain requires a reliable delivery system at project and school level' (Stringfield *et al.*, 2001: 36). It is clear that success with HRS relies on schools adopting the model fully without the possibility of modification.

Slavin's 'Success for All' project (Slavin *et al.* 1994, 1996) and Joyce's 'Models of Teaching' approach (Joyce *et al.*, 1999) are similarly highly prescriptive. Both 'Success For All' and 'Models of Teaching' stand out as highly effective approaches of school improvement. Both approaches have been carefully and systematically evaluated over a number of years and a substantial evidence base exists to support their positive impact on schools in the US and other countries.

All these programmes have proved to be highly effective because schools have actively sought to match the developmental needs of the school with the particular strategy or school improvement approach. Hopkins *et al.* (1997: 8) highlight the need for a 'fit' between programme and the developmental needs of the school. They categorise school improvement strategies into different types as follows.

Type 1

Strategies that assist failing schools to become moderately effective. They need to involve a high level of external support. Failing schools cannot improve themselves. These strategies have to involve a clear and direct focus on a limited number of basic curriculum and organisational issues in order to build the confidence and competence to continue. These strategies usually involve a certain level of external support and intervention. Examples of such school improvement strategies would be 'Success for All' (Slavin *et al.* 1994, 1996), Joyce's 'Models of Teaching' approach (Joyce and Weil 1996) and the High Reliability Project.

Type 2

Strategies that assist moderately effective schools to become effective. These strategies do not rely as heavily on external support but tend to be more school-initiated. Strategic school improvement programmes such as the 'Improving the Quality of Education for All' (IQEA) project or the Accelerated Schools Project are pertinent examples.

Type 3

Strategies that assist effective schools to remain so. In these instances external support, although often welcomed, is not necessary as the school searches out and creates its own support networks. Exposure to new ideas and practices, collaboration through consortia or 'pairing' type arrangements seem to be common in these situations. Examples of these types of school improvement strategies would be school improvement projects such as the League of Professional Schools (Glickman, 1990) or the Coalition of Essential Schools (Sizer, 1992).

Within the range of school improvement programmes that impact positively upon schools and students, the degree of external intervention varies quite considerably. Type 1 strategies incorporate high levels of external support and engagement while type 3 strategies are premised upon schools supporting themselves through networks or other groupings. For less effective schools the school improvement approach needs to be tightly defined and fairly prescriptive. In schools that are effective or improving the strategies adopted can be loosely defined and structured. As noted in the previous chapter, the key to school improvement lies in selecting the programme or approach that matches the developmental needs or priorities of the school.

REFLECTION

Consider the type 1, type 2 and type 3 strategies:
What improvement strategies is your school currently implementing?
How far do they reflect one of the three types?
What does this imply about your school and its current improvement work?

Characteristics of effective school improvement

Despite differences of approach, highly effective school improvement projects have been found to share certain characteristics or features.

A broad comparative analysis of highly successful programmes demonstrates a number of shared principles or features (Harris, 2000c). This analysis found that effective school improvement programmes:

- focus closely on classroom improvement;
- utilise discrete instructional or pedagogical strategies, i.e. they are explicit in the models of teaching they prescribe;
- apply pressure at the implementation stage to ensure adherence to the programme;
- collect systematic evaluative evidence about the impact upon schools and classrooms;
- mobilise change at a numbers of levels within the organisation, e.g. classroom, department, teacher level;
- generate cultural as well as structural change;
- engage teachers in professional dialogue and development;
- provide external agency and support.

This comparison showed that while the school improvement programmes and projects varied in terms of content, nature and approach they reflected a similar philosophy. Central to this philosophy is an adherence to the school as the centre of change and the teacher as the catalyst for classroom change and development. Within highly effective school improvement programmes the non-negotiable elements are a focus on teaching and learning, a commitment to professional development and diffused or devolved leadership.

While new school improvement projects and initiatives seem to emerge daily, evidence concerning their impact is not always forthcoming. Critics of the school improvement field have highlighted the relative absence of evaluative evidence concerning the impact of school improvement upon student performance and achievement. In addition, there has been little consideration of the relative effectiveness of different school improvement initiatives in enhancing student performance. The studies that do exist offer little evidence concerning the relative effectiveness of one approach over another.

Further comparative studies of school improvement are needed to assist schools in selecting improvement programmes that are most effective and 'fit' their developmental needs. At present, there is an accumulating knowledge base about school improvement arising from the numerous projects and programmes around the world. This knowledge base has provided important insights into the process of improvement and there are some common components of successful school improvement.

Vision-building

A large number of school improvement projects require schools to share in a vision of where the school could be, or that they generate their own vision with support and help from external agents. The evidence would suggest that the possibilities for school improvement are extended if there is clear vision linked to high-quality support. It also suggests that this vision needs to be shared and regularly reconfirmed as the process of change takes place. Conversely, the absence of a clear vision has shown to lead to confusion, demoralisation and failure within much school improvement work.

Extended leadership

At the core of any school improvement effort is a whole new way of teachers and management working together. In schools engaged in school improvement, both senior managers and teachers have to function as leaders and decision-makers as they attempt to bring about fundamental changes. Essentially, school improvement necessitates a reconceptualisation of leadership where teachers and managers engage in shared decision-making and risk-taking. The emphasis is upon active and participatory leadership in school improvement work, rather than top-down delegation.

Programme fit

There are many different programmes for school improvement in existence, but no one 'blueprint for action'. The research shows that there is no universal starting point for any school. In each individual school context, history, leadership, staffing, incentives and personal history will vary. All these factors play a considerable role in school improvement and highlight the importance of selecting the school improvement programme that best 'fits' the individual school needs and situation. However, in most cases schools choose programmes without consideration or knowledge of the alternatives.

Focus on students

What distinguishes the school improvement movement from other school reform efforts is the understanding that it is necessary to focus upon student outcomes in academic performance as the key success criteria, rather than teacher perceptions of the innovation. Highly successful school improvement projects have been shown to place an 'emphasis upon specific learning outcomes rather than general learning goals' (Hopkins, 2001: 71). Where school improvement works most effectively, it involves teachers aiming for a clearly defined set of learning outcomes or targets. Within successful school improvement, the learning level is the main focus for development and change. Hence, within successful projects there is an emphasis upon well-defined student learning outcomes along with the provision of clear instructional frameworks.

Multi-level intervention

Much early school improvement work tended to concentrate upon school-level change. However, subsequent work has recognised the importance of encouraging school-level, teacher-level and classroom-level change. Consequently, a multi-level approach is now part of the most effective school improvement programmes. This necessitates using all initiators, promoters and activists within the change process at all levels, both externally and internally.

Instructionally driven

Within a number of highly effective school improvement projects there is a clear articulation of the instructional framework that guides the development activity at the classroom level. In 'Success for All', for example, the instructional framework comes from the research base concerning cooperative learning. A range of classroom strategies are used within the project such as 'think pair share' and 'peer tutoring', both directly derived from the cooperative learning literature. In IQEA

Joyce and Weil's (1996) models of teaching provide the cornerstone for the developmental work in schools. Schools are encouraged to work on one model at a time and adopt Joyce's (1988) approach to staff development that encompasses demonstration, practice, observation and feedback. Across all the projects, an instructional framework provides the teaching strategies and approaches required to secure improved student outcomes.

External agency

Evaluative evidence illustrates that school improvement cannot progress very far without the influence of external and internal 'agency'. Earl and Lee (1998: 3) describe successful school improvement as a chain reaction of 'urgency, energy, agency and more energy'. Their work suggests that building the capacity for school improvement requires both internal and external forces for change and development.

Investing in teaching

Teacher development is a major component of all successful school improvement programmes. Research has shown that professional development is usually most effective when it is not delivered by extraneous experts in off-site locations but when it is embedded in the school and when it is the focus of collaborative discussion and action (Little, 1993). In a large number of the programmes, staff development is school-based and classroom-focused. The main thrust of the work with teachers in each of the projects is to equip them to manage classroom change, development and improvement.

Building professional communities

In a number of the projects (e.g. Accelerated Schools, IQEA) teachers are actively encouraged to build their own professional communities both within and outside the school. Emphasis is placed upon teacher collaboration and networking. The net result of this activity is not only the sharing of good practice but also the establishing of professional development communities within the school that can sustain and maintain development.

Enquiry-led

The importance of enquiry and reflection within the process of school improvement has long been established. Levine and Lezotte (1990) noted that a 'commitment to inquiry' was a consistent feature of highly effective schools. The analysis and application of research findings by teachers as part of their routine professional activity has been shown to have had a positive effect upon the quality of teaching and learning (Harris and Hopkins, 1997; 1999). There is evidence from highly successful school improvement projects that providing teachers with the opportunity to enquire into their practice has resulted in changed attitudes, beliefs and behaviours. Moreover, these changes in attitudes, beliefs and behaviours have directly affected their classroom teaching and resulted in improved learning outcomes for students.

All successful school improvement involves some form of change and requires schools to manage and implement the change process. In order to ensure that change is fully implemented, schools have to put in place the necessary systems, processes and structures. It is clear that the most effective school improvement programmes assist schools to 'build the capacity' for implementing change and improvement. In other words, through a combination of pressure and support they are able to assist schools in generating both the *readiness to change* and the *internal capacity* to manage the change process. The next chapter considers the process of managing and evaluating change.

QUESTIONS FOR FURTHER EXPLORATION

This chapter suggests that effective school improvement programmes:

- focus closely on classroom improvement;
- utilise discrete instructional or pedagogical strategies, i.e. they are explicit in the models of teaching they prescribe;
- apply pressure at the implementation stage to ensure adherence to the programme;

- collect systematic evaluative evidence about the impact upon schools and classrooms;
- mobilise change at a number of levels within the organisation, e.g. classroom, department, teacher level;
- generate cultural as well as structural change;
- engage teachers in professional dialogue and development;
- provide external agency and support.

How far does this list reflect the school improvement activity within your own school?

What elements are missing from your current school improvement work?

In what ways could these be addressed?

3 Changing and improving schools

Introduction

The process of school improvement inevitably involves some form of change. It is important to remember, however, that 'not all change leads to school improvement' (Fullan, 1991: 3). Some changes can actually be counter-productive to school development or are so complex that they prove impossible to implement. Superficial change can also be a distraction and a way of avoiding serious developmental work. Within schools that are improving there usually exists a 'climate for change' or 'a climate for improvement'. This essentially means that the school is committed to improvement and is prepared to engage in cultural change. Developing this climate has been found to be a necessary prerequisite of effective change at the level of the school. Schools that have been shown to be improving are those that have carefully selected the changes they wish to make and have a means of implementing those changes. In order to manage change effectively, schools need to understand the nature and process of change. They also need to understand why barriers to change might occur.

A major reason for the failure of change lies in a lack of careful attention to the process of change. While the instigation of change is relatively straightforward, the subsequent interpretation and implementation of any change is much more difficult. As Fullan (1991: 65) has summarised, 'educational change is technically simple and socially complex'. While the rationale for change may be clear, its manifestation within a school may create difficulties because of the social processes involved.

Change itself is a complex phenomenon that needs to be understood by those intending to instigate change. Hopkins *et al.* (1996: 2) suggest that change tends to manifest itself in two distinctive ways within a school organisation. The first way is 'incremental change that is a gradual and sometimes subtle transition from one state to another. Here the change process may occur as the result of internal factors such as changes in personnel, or external factors such as a change in the statutory curriculum requirements. This form of change is gradual, unintended and rarely involves planning.'

In contrast, the second way in which change manifests itself within a school is in the form of *planned change*. Planned change deliberately seeks to alter and interrupt the natural course of events (Fullan, 1991). It is a conscious intervention that is purposive, aiming to create a new order or to establish a new set of practices. In school improvement activity the dominant form of change is planned change where deliberate attempts are made to change practice or alter behaviours. Successful school improvement involves careful planning for the proposed change and the anticipation of problems or barriers before the change is introduced. It is important that those involved in the change consider the impact it is likely to have upon others.

REFLECTION

Think about a change that you were involved in that was successful. What contributed to its success? Think about a change that you were involved in that was unsuccessful. What contributed to its failure? On reflection how important were people's responses to change in both situations?

Responses to change

Fullan (1991) suggests that at the crux of change is how individuals respond to and experience the proposed change. Very rarely do those proposing change or introducing change think about what it means to others at a *personal* level. Yet, how others feel about the change is a critical determinant of how they will ultimately respond to it. Fullan

(2001: 1) notes that 'if you ask people to brainstorm change, they come up with a mixture of negative and positive terms. On the one side, fear, anxiety, loss, danger, panic and on the other, exhilaration, risk-taking, excitement, improvements, energising. For better or worse, change arouses emotions.' Consequently, the feelings aroused by and concerning any proposed changes need to be carefully considered. If insufficient attention is paid to the emotional responses to change this may result in the change being undermined or deliberately blocked.

When considering the responses of others to change it is important to remember the difference between voluntary and imposed change. Changes that are imposed without consultation are most likely to incur resistance and sabotage. Conversely change that is self-imposed or voluntary is more likely to succeed simply because individuals feel involved and have some power within the situation. For those leading change in schools it is important to remember how others are likely to respond if they feel uninvolved or not consulted about the proposed change. For most people, a common response to any change is to feel loss, anxiety and struggle. This is both a natural and necessary part of the change process.

Negative responses to change may be misinterpreted by those leading change as recalcitrance or resistance to the additional work that will be involved. However, it may be that those asked to undertake the change are feeling pressurised or frustrated at the imposition of something new without any consultation. Whatever the origin of feelings of resentment or resistance, if they are not discussed openly this will make the proposed change even more difficult to implement. Consequently, the way that change is presented to others is critically important and will determine the degree of resistance or support that will ensue.

If there is continued resistance to change, despite presenting the rationale for it very clearly, the real source of the resistance needs to be discovered. For some teachers, the proposed change may leave them feeling vulnerable or apprehensive. For other teachers the increased work involved in the change might leave them feeling pressurised and stressed. For those leading change within the school it is important that the purpose of change is understood, that the implications of the change are clear and generally accepted and that adequate support is in place. Managing change successfully involves the anticipation of the possible responses from others prior to introducing the change. It also necessitates considering the proposed change in some depth before sharing it more widely with others. The following questions need to be considered before introducing the change:

- How important is this change?
- How necessary is this change at this time?
- What priority does the change have?
- How will others view this change and respond to it?
- What will be the main benefits from this change?

By considering these questions before introducing a new development, greater control of the change process is secured. It is also important to consider what type of change is being proposed. Changes can vary according to degree of imposition and the time-scale proposed:

- imposed and without choice of time-scale, e.g. National Literacy Strategy;
- imposed but with some choice of timing, e.g. performance management;
- desirable with choice of timing, e.g. school improvement;
- essential with no choice of timing, e.g. OFSTED action plan.

Some further factors that need to be considered for each change are the degree to which the change will require new systems, practices or behaviours, i.e. *change as replacement* or whether the changes planned will simply refine or alter existing systems, practices, behaviours, i.e. *change as modification*. Bennis (1969) proposes three approaches to change:

- *Power coercive*: where organisational members are put under great psychological pressure to change;
- *Rational empirical*: where organisational members are presented with the rational and logical reasons for change;
- *Normative/Re-educative*: where organisational members are encouraged through emotive and personal means to engage in the process of change.

These approaches are not mutually exclusive but should be viewed as a range of different ways in which change could be introduced. In preparing for the introduction of change it is important to plan in order to be able to manage the process most effectively.

Planning for change

In planning for change it is important to understand the different phases associated with the change process. To manage change effectively means anticipating the difficulties and requirements at each phase. Even though the change process may be thought of as linear and rational, in reality it is often a complex and highly emotive activity. Hence, it is important that all those engaged in managing the change process are familiar with the three phases of change. Fullan (1991) has identified three phases of the change process:

- the initiation phase
- the implementation phase
- the institutionalisation or continuation phase.

Lewin (1947) similarly viewed change as a three-stage process but described the change process using the following terms:

- unfreezing
- moving
- refreezing.

It is his view that in order for change to be most effective the present state has to be sufficiently 'unfrozen' or change will not occur. This means that schools have to be ready to embark upon the change process and that the present state has to be one where change is possible. Schein (1992) talks about three stages in the unfreezing process. These are:

1 presence of evidence of a problem
2 connection of this problem with the organisation's purpose
3 a possible solution.

It is suggested that if these three stages are undertaken, the 'unfreezing' will commence. Another means of assessing a school's readiness or capability to change and improve is through initial diagnosis. Within the 'Improving the Quality of Education for All' school improvement project (IQEA) schools have to complete a 'conditions scale' which provides them with some base-line data about their internal capacity to undertake school improvement (Hopkins *et al.*, 1996). This data offers the school some indication of their 'readiness state' to undertake change or whether some 'unfreezing' is still required.

Whatever terms are used to describe the change process, it is clear that all effective change involves starting change, securing change and sustaining change. These three phases merge together as change progresses. These three phases are not mutually exclusive but are overlapping and intrinsically linked. There is no prescribed time-scale for each phase because the pace of change differs according to context. Change is approached differently in different contexts. Innovations need to be sufficiently flexible for schools to adapt them for their own circumstances and situations. Also, change rarely involves a single activity or act. Any innovation will inevitably lead to other changes and have a range of consequences. Sarason (1990: 5) has described this as the 'rippling effect' where change inevitably generates a whole range of intended and unintended outcomes.

In order to manage the change process effectively it is important to understand what each phase involves and to consider how the phases interact. School improvement will require those leading the process of change to be familiar with the phases of change. It will also require setting a realistic time-scale for the proposed change. If change is introduced too quickly or without adequate time for proper implementation, it is likely to flounder and fail. Even small-scale change takes time and requires that careful attention be paid to the phases of change.

Starting change

The 'starting phase' is the point at which the proposed change is conceptualised and introduced. There may be various routes to reaching this stage. For example, the proposed change may emerge from a whole-school review, be imposed by external agencies or result from a problem within the school. The origin of the change is important because it will have a direct effect on the way in which the change is introduced and understood (Hopkins *et al.*, 1996). There is no one way or best way to commence the process of change. Schools become involved in improvement activities in a variety of ways. Joyce (1990: 16) uses the metaphor of 'doors to improvement' to describe how schools become involved. He delineates between external doors and internal doors to change and improvement.

External doors that lead to change and improvement include:

* inspection
* performance management
* league tables
* test scores.

Internal doors that lead to change and improvement include:

* self-evaluation
* leadership change
* research evidence
* school development planning.

Whatever doors lead to school improvement, it is important that the focus for improvement is meaningful to teachers. In managing change it is important to anticipate how teachers will view the change and what barriers they might present to the change. 'Improvement efforts which duck the question of what's in it for teachers are likely to fail' (Gray and Wilcox, 1995: 250).

There are many variables influencing both if and how a change is introduced. Fullan (1991) has identified a range of barriers that affect the successful initiation of change. There are two barriers of direct relevance to those managing change. The first barrier to change is the lack of access to information about the change itself. For many teachers change is something usually imposed from above or externally generated, e.g. National Literacy Strategy. As a result they are rarely given the opportunity to share in the decision-making processes that have led to the change. Where teachers are kept informed of proposed changes and are part of the decision-making process a greater sense of commitment and support for the change is generated (Fullan, 1991; Hargreaves, 1994). It may not always be possible to keep all teachers fully informed of every discussion or development but where important and major changes are concerned access to information is important.

A second potential barrier to the initiation of change is the competing pressure and demands upon teachers' time. In recent years, increased curriculum demands upon teachers in the UK have meant that they have less time to meet with one another to discuss new ideas. The research evidence demonstrates the potency of teachers working together but also indicates that teachers have less and less time to do so (Day, 1999). It is clear that school development and improvement occurs when teachers:

- engage in frequent, continuous and concrete talk about teaching practice;
- frequently observe and provide feedback to each other;
- plan, design and evaluate teaching materials together (Little, 1993).

Where such norms of collaborative practice are not in place, innovation and the initiation of change become more difficult to achieve. The initiation phase involves everything that happens in preparation for the change to take place. This is the opportunity for those involved in the change to prepare by seeking advice, support and guidance. This preparation is vitally important if change is to be properly implemented.

Securing change

Whether or not a change happens in practice is largely dependent upon the quality of implementation. This is the phase where the change or innovation is put into practice. It is the stage where planning stops and where action commences. For a large number of innovations this is where change flounders and loses momentum. Fullan (1991) calls this the 'implementation dip' and suggests that there are numerous factors that causally influence implementation and contribute to the process of successful change. These factors include:

- clarity of purpose;
- shared purpose;
- clear outcomes;
- forward planning;
- external support;
- evaluative feedback.

During the implementation phase there will be a need for a combination of *pressure* on and *support* for teachers. There has to be enough pressure to ensure that the momentum of change continues and that action takes place. Conversely, there needs to be technical, emotional and professional support to ensure that team members feel equipped to take on the tasks related to the change (Stoll and Fink, 1996). If there is too much pressure, then stress will result. If there is too much support, then complacency will follow. It is important to retain a balance between pressure and support in order to secure change and to move through the implementation phase.

During the implementation phase there will be a crucial time when the change appears to be making little progress. Fullan (2001: 40) notes that 'one of our most consistent findings and understandings about the change process in education is that all schools experience "implementation dips". The implementation dip is literally a dip in performance and confidence as one encounters an innovation that requires new skills and new understandings.' This 'implementation dip' is inevitable in any change process and is experienced as a general feeling that the change is making little or no progress. This is an intrinsic part of the change process and does not mean that the change has failed. Instead, it indicates that the change is at a critical stage and that additional effort is required to mobilise the change.

In some respects, things will get worse before they get better as people grapple with redefining and reshaping behaviour and practices as part of the change (Joyce and Showers, 1988). Fullan (2001: 41) suggests that during the *implementation dip* people experience two kinds of problems. Firstly, they experience fear of change and a feeling of being out of control. Secondly, they feel an absence of the skills and abilities required to implement the change. He suggests that effective leaders support others through the implementation dip by offering technical, emotional and physical support. It is also evident that successful implementation is secured by certain factors being in place.

The key success factors at the implementation phase are:

- clarity about the purposes and intentions of the change;
- shared control over implementation, i.e. team responsibility;
- an appropriate mix of pressure and support;
- early evidence of success;

- sustained enthusiasm;
- will, skill and persistence.

With each successive change, those involved in managing the change process will become more skilled. The experience of change will provide a basis upon which to plan and implement more complex changes. It is important that early changes are small, manageable and successful. This will encourage others to embark upon more complex or sophisticated change. The goal of the school change is to modify the existing culture so that improvements can take place. Where change is fully implemented it is no longer viewed as a new or separate development.

Sustaining change

In generating change for school improvement one of the most difficult tasks is to sustain change over time. It is fairly easy to initiate change but much more difficult to sustain change. The continuation or institutionalisation phase is the point at which change is not regarded as being anything new because it has been embedded into the systems and culture of the school. It has become an established part of everyday practice within the school. While it might be assumed that this will happen automatically, in practice it requires that the change is monitored and evaluated to ensure that it is making the intended impact and that this impact is sustained. As Huberman and Miles note:

> Innovations are highly perishable goods. Taking continuation for granted assuming magically that it will happen by itself, or will necessarily result from a technically mastered, demonstrably effective project – is naïve and usually self defeating.
>
> (1984: 14)

Building the capacity for school improvement necessitates that change is carefully planned and managed. It also requires monitoring the extent of change and its impact. An important role for those leading change is to manage and control overload. A school that is constantly changing or developing will have little time for consolidating change. Fullan (2001: 35) talks about 'Christmas Tree Schools' which have so many innovations that they 'glitter from a distance'. Unfortunately, schools that acquire initiative after initiative end up 'superficially adorned with many decorations, lacking depth and coherence' (Fullan, 2001: 35). Therefore, there needs to be time set aside for a school to embed the change and to evaluate the change fully before moving on to the next new development. In this way change will be less of a 'conveyor belt' approach to school improvement and much more a strategy for changing school culture.

Evaluating change

School evaluation is an important link in the modification or reshaping of school culture. It provides the critical feedback and information flow that will enable those within a school to reflect upon changes and to modify practices. At the heart of school improvement is the process of self-reflection and self-evaluation. The typical evaluation cycle of review, planning and action is an essential part of successful development and change. Dalin (1998: 240) suggests that evaluation should evaluate a specific activity and that it must be related to the schools' internal self-review process.

Before embarking upon evaluation for school improvement schools should consider:

- What aspect of this change do we want to evaluate?
- What information will we need?
- When will the evaluation be undertaken?
- Who will be involved?
- How will the findings be shared and disseminated?
- How do we ensure that the evaluation leads to action?

An important dimension of managing the change process is judging whether, and to what extent, the change has fulfilled its intentions. Gauging the impact of change is difficult without the existence of clear targets and, by association, requires evidence or feedback about progress towards these targets. Hence school self-evaluation provides a basis upon which judgements and informed decisions are made concerning future improvement. Southworth and Conner (1999) suggest that an evaluation needs to be:

- comprehensive;
- systematic;
- objective;
- reliable.

It has to be comprehensive insofar as it collects a range of data on the development or change. It has to be systematic in the way the data is collected and as far as possible to look at the evidence in an impartial and objective way. Finally, the data collected needs to be reliable in order to substantiate and validate the subsequent judgements.

Some evaluative questions that might be asked at the outset of change are:

- Is the proposed change or development necessary at this time?
- Does the proposed change or development build upon the school's strengths?
- Are sufficient resources available to support the proposed change or development? Are additional resources required?
- What will be the benefits of the proposed change or development?
- How will these benefits be monitored and evaluated?

At the implementation phase the evaluation process concentrates upon providing evidence of the impact of change and highlighting any barriers or difficulties incurred as the change becomes embedded in this institution. Some evaluative questions that might be asked at the implementation stage are as follows:

- How well is the change or development being introduced?
- What are the indicators of success to date?
- What are the major barriers? How might these be overcome?
- Are any changes or modifications required? How might these be introduced?
- What balance of pressure and support is now needed to sustain the change or development?

The purpose of the evaluation is to make some judgements about the overall impact or effect of the change or development. The types of questions that can inform judgements at the continuation phase are as follows:

- What have been the main outcomes from the change or development?
- Have there been any unintended outcomes?
- To what extent has the change or development improved work within the school?
- What further changes should be made?

An evidence-based approach to managing change is vital to successful school improvement. Collecting evidence can be time consuming so it is important that the evidence that is collected provides the basis for making a judgement on the evaluation issue or question. There are a variety of data collection methods that can be used for evaluative purposes. They each have various advantages and disadvantages. A summary of data collection methods is shown in Table 3.1.

Hopkins (1995) has argued for 'more user friendly yet penetrating techniques' to investigate and measure the complexity of the school change and improvement process. While it is important to evaluate change it is also important not to make the evaluation task overly burdensome by devising and using too many data-collection tools. It is important to select the most appropriate method and to ensure that it will provide the type of information that will prove most useful in making judgements about the impact of change.

It is important that whatever data is collected is manageable and useable. In order to make a judgement about the impact of a change or development the data needs to be reliable and valid. Improving schools means investing in forms of data collection and analysis that will provide reliable feedback to inform new developments. To be most effective evaluation needs to be built into the process of development to ensure that the impact of change is fully captured. School self-evaluation is an important means of gauging improvement and change but it is also a powerful mechanism for building the capacity for change and development. The next chapter will consider other ways in which schools can build the capacity for change and improvement.

Table 3.1 Summary of evaluation tools

Tool	Advantages	Disadvantages	Particular uses
Interview	Allows for an in-depth response from various informants, i.e. students, teachers, governors, etc.	Time-consuming. Analysis can prove difficult.	To obtain information which would not be easily obtained from a questionnaire, e.g. sensitive, personal information.
Audio-tape recording	Provides a complete record of a conversation or interview.	Can often inhibit individuals from giving certain kinds of information.	To obtain complete records and detailed evidence.
Video-tape	Provides visual information	Can often be inhibitive. Can prove expensive and difficult to organise.	To obtain information which can be used later in a diagramatic way. A complete visual record.
Questionnaire	Can reach large numbers of respondents. Can provide both quantitative and qualitative data.	Return rate can often be low and the information collected may be of little value.	To obtain specific information and feedback from a potentially large number of people.
Survey	Can yield an enormous amount of information in a very economic way.	Not very flexible. Time-consuming to conduct.	Appropriate when large samples are involved.
Observation	Can reveal characteristics of group or individuals that would be difficult to obtain by other means.	Time-consuming and subjective.	Appropriate for looking at teacher–student relationships or interaction in the classroom.
Logs, diaries	Quick and easy to produce. Can provide in-depth information.	Time-consuming to keep and analyse.	For obtaining insight into students' views or ideas about an initiative.

Source: Busher and Harris (2000)

QUESTIONS FOR FURTHER EXPLORATION

At the core of school improvement is the process of change. This has to be managed carefully. Think about a change that is currently being implemented in your school:

- Who initiated the change? Did it meet with resistance?
- What is the current view of the change? How far are people cooperating?
- How will you overcome the implementation dip? How will you remove barriers to change?
- How will the success of the change be judged?
- How will you tell whether the change has made a difference to students?

4 Building the capacity for school improvement

Introduction

School improvement has been defined as 'an approach to educational change that has the twin purposes of enhancing student achievement and strengthening the school's capacity for change' (Hopkins *et al.*, 1994: 68). If the ultimate goal of school improvement is to enhance students' progress and achievement, research shows that this is best achieved when schools extend their own capacity for development. Within the context of school improvement capacity is the ability to enable all students to reach higher standards. Capacity may be built by improving the performance of teachers, adding more resources, materials or technology and by restructuring how tasks are undertaken. Most capacity-building strategies in schools target individual teachers. As Sergiovanni points out:

> Teachers count in helping schools to be effective. Building capacity among teachers and focusing that capacity on students and their learning is the crucial factor. Continuous capacity building and continuous focusing is best done within communities of practice.
>
> (2000: 140)

Wenger (1998) suggests that individuals derive their understanding of their work from the community of practice within which they carry it out. The members of the community have a shared understanding of the work and individuals are drawn into the community by a process of learning where the boundaries are what define the collection of tasks that make up the practice.

There are two important points about communities of practice. First, everyone is a member of more than one community of practice. Teachers, for example, are part of a wider community of teachers, which defines certain aspects of behaviour as legitimate, whilst also being members of a school. Second, teachers are simultaneously members of a school, a subject area and an individual classroom. Through this multiple membership individuals transact the expectations of one community of practice into others.

Different communities of practice, even within the same organisation, may have quite different perceptions of what counts as 'best' or even 'good' practice. Wenger (1998) suggests that individuals derive their identity from their membership of, and participation in, communities of practice. Consequently, to simply operate on the basis of 'the school' or even 'the department' as a unit of analysis is to ignore these potentially profound meanings which individuals invest in their day-to-day actions. This suggests that a more negotiative, more flexible, and less directive approach to determining the criteria for assessing school improvement is required. Professional community is one where teachers participate in decision-making, have a shared sense of purpose, engage in collaborative work and accept joint responsibility for the outcomes of their work. 'Building capacity among teachers and focusing that capacity on students and their learning is the crucial factor' (Sergiovanni, 2000).

Capacity-building from a relatively simple perspective is creating the experiences and opportunities for people to learn how to do things together. Internal capacity 'is the power to engage in and sustain continuous learning of teachers and the school itself for the purpose of enhancing student learning' (Stoll, 1999).

Discussions of teacher capacity often focus upon their knowledge and skills. However, there are other areas of teacher capacity that are vital. Studies suggest that the capacity to teach in different ways is directly connected to views of self, to teachers' beliefs about their role in classroom activity and to the personas they adopt in the classroom. Implementing change also requires a disposition to meet new standards for student learning and to make necessary changes in practice. One important disposition involves teachers' attitudes to subject-matter as well as towards students' expectations concerning achievement.

Research evidence from the most successful school improvement projects emphasises the importance of fostering the development capacity of the school. To build capacity for change and development requires that certain conditions are in place at school- and classroom-level. Work by Hopkins *et al.* (1996; 1997; 2000) has identified a number of school- and classroom-level conditions that contribute directly to building organisational capacity. These 'conditions' at school and classroom level mutually support and sustain school improvement.

The school- and classroom-level conditions 'are the infra-structural elements and processes that directly impact upon the way in which change is initiated and managed within the school' (Hopkins *et al.*, 1997: 24). At school level, these conditions are important in generating a climate where change and innovation can be implemented. Hopkins *et al.* (2000: 7) have identified the following set of school-level conditions:

- a commitment to staff development;
- practical efforts to involve staff, students and the community in school policies and decisions;
- 'transformational' leadership approaches;
- effective coordination strategies;
- proper attention to the potential benefits of enquiry and reflection;
- a commitment to collaborative planning activity.

At the classroom level also Hopkins *et al.* (1997:) have developed a set of conditions that facilitate and sustain effective teaching and learning. These classroom conditions are as follows:

- *Authentic relationships*: being the quality, openness and congruence of relationships existing in the classroom.
- *Rules and boundaries*: being the pattern of expectations set by the teacher and school of student performance and behaviour within the classroom.
- *Planning, resources and preparation*: the access of teachers to a range of pertinent teaching materials and the ability to plan and differentiate these materials for a range of students.
- *Teacher's repertoire*: the range of teaching styles and models internalised and available to a teacher dependent on student, context, curriculum and desired outcome.
- *Pedagogic partnerships*: the ability of teachers to form professional relationships within and outside the classroom that focus on the study and improvement of practice.

- *Reflection on teaching*: the capacity of the individual teacher to reflect on his/her own practice, and to put to the test of practice, specifications of teaching from other sources.

REFLECTION

How could these classroom conditions be shared with teachers in your school?
Could they be used as a basis for talking about classroom improvement?

By working upon both sets of conditions simultaneously (i.e. school level and classroom level) there is the potential to build capacity within and across the organisation. These conditions have been shown to be centrally important in school development. They need to be fostered to create and sustain the capacity for school improvement. Focusing upon these conditions means taking a radically different view of the school as an organisation. The traditional view of schools is of a hierarchy operating in a rational way with the headteacher at the apex of the organisation. Taking this view, control and power reside at the top and roles are clearly demarcated. In this bureaucratic model, the school is viewed in a mechanistic way with change being directed from the top and transacted through the various layers of the organisation.

This mechanistic view of the school implies an approach to improvement that is both rational and structural in orientation. The limitations of this approach have been highlighted already and it is clear that an alternative view of the school as an organisation is required. Morgan notes:

As we look around the organisational world we begin to see that it is possible to identify different species of organisation in different kinds of environments. We find that bureaucratic organisations tend to work most effectively in environments that are stable or protected in some way and that very different species are found in more turbulent regions.

(1997: 33)

Within the more turbulent or complex environments, effective change is premised upon a view of the organisation as a 'living or open system' (Morgan, 1997: 44). Within living or open systems, the organisation can adapt to environmental circumstances and changes through a modification of its internal conditions. Consequently, this view of organisational change means that by enhancing their internal conditions schools can build the capacity for change and development.

Building capacity

Research has shown that successful schools are committed to improvement and are prepared to change existing practices. Without this commitment schools will adapt and modify existing practices. A 'climate for change' can be influenced by the school leader and can be 'set' by the particular leadership style adopted. School leaders need to have a clear vision for the development of the school and an ability to share this vision with colleagues to ensure that developments are taken forward. Where leadership is too authoritarian, or alternatively too *laissez-faire*, development will not occur and improvement will be difficult to achieve (Harris, 1998).

One of the most striking findings from the various school improvement studies has been the collegiate vision adopted by schools. Improving schools are marked by a constant interchange of professional information at both a formal and an informal level. Similarly, schools that are improving seem to have ways of working that encourage staff, governors, parents and students to feel involved. These ways of working provide support for the school's improvement efforts.

In order to generate involvement within a school, clear communication systems have to be in place. To achieve optimum levels of involvement, information flows have to be transparent. Where communication is unclear, or muddled, there is evidence to show that this restricts effective collaboration (Harris, 1998). There should be opportunities for consultation and staff participation in decision-making for school improvement to occur. By providing such opportunities, feelings of involvement should increase to build a sense of community and a commitment to improving standards.

Across schools the ability to organise key elements of teaching and learning in an optimum way is essential. This requires coordination to ensure that key tasks are undertaken efficiently. As schools are busy places and there are numerous developments occurring at once, the need for coordination is of paramount importance. This will necessitate delegating some core tasks and activities and establishing systems of communication to ensure that these activities are coordinated.

Within the school improvement literature, planning has been shown to be an important factor. Besides helping the school organise what it is already doing and what it needs to do in a more purposeful and coherent way, effective planning is about helping teachers manage innovation and change successfully. There have been a number of studies that have focused on the impact of planning on schools, teachers and classrooms. Research suggests that although many schools have development plans they do not always lead to school improvement. Hargreaves and Hopkins (1994: 14) suggest 'that the organisational and cultural arrangements of the school predispose it to certain types of plan, and that there can be a dialectical relationship between the plan and the organisational and cultural conditions of the school'. Therefore, planning offers a 'map' for improvement that will require operational-ising if improvements are to occur.

Ultimately the success of a school depends upon the success teachers have in working with their respective classes. There is a body of evidence that demonstrates that teachers work most effectively when they are supported by other teachers and work collegially (Hargreaves, 1994). Collegial relations and collective practice are at the core of building the capacity for school improvement. In schools that are failing the quality of relationships between teachers will almost inevitably require most immediate attention. The quality of relationships rather than resources or systems enables schools to develop and grow. It is the nature of communication between those working together on a daily basis that offers the best indicator of organisational health. Hopkins *et al.* note that

> successful schools encourage co-ordination by creating collabo-rative environments which encourages involvement, professional development, mutual support and assistance in problem solving.
>
> (1996: 177)

If sustained improvement is to be achieved, teacher partnerships and other forms of collaboration should be encouraged. This implies a form of professional development and learning that is premised upon collaboration, cooperation and networking. It implies a view of the school as a learning community where teachers and students learn together.

The importance of teacher development within school improvement has long been established. It is also clear that teachers develop through enquiry into and reflection upon their own practice. Hopkins *et al.* (1996) point to the fact that school improvement is a process that is data-driven and engages teachers in personal reflection. Schools that are failing tend to be characterised by an impoverishment in teaching and teacher development. They are schools where there is a culture of individualism and where the process of teaching is rarely evaluated or discussed.

Building capacity for school improvement implies a profound change in schools as organisations. Sackney *et al.* argue that

> the post-modern era suggests a conception of organisations as processes and relationships rather than as structures and rules with conversation as the central medium for the creation of both individual meaning and organisational change. From this perspective, the image of schools as learning organisations seems like a promising response to the continuing demands for re-structuring.
>
> (1998: 52)

This suggests a view of the school as a professional community where teachers have the opportunity to learn from one another and to work together. In such communities leadership is distributed throughout the system and improvement 'occurs from an internal search for meaning, relevance and connection' (Mitchell and Sackney, 2000: 139). Barth (1990) talks about creating a community of learners where the prime purpose of the organisation is to increase the capacity to bring about collective growth and development.

Building capacity for improvement involves pulling the main levers for change and development within a school. Capacity building will obviously differ from school to school and from context to context. However, without a focus upon building the capacity for change, the chances of sustained innovation and improvement are substantially lessened. More importantly, the possibility of raising student performance and achievement becomes even more remote.

Of central importance in building learning capacity within organisations is the human perspective rather than the system perspective. By placing people at the centre of change and development there is greater opportunity for organisational growth. Building capacity means extending the potential and capabilities of individuals and means investing in professional development. The metaphor of the learning community encapsulates the importance of fostering and harnessing the learning of all individuals: parents, students, governors and teachers. This can only be achieved with external support and help. While it is possible for schools to improve themselves, it is also important to recognise that building the capacity for learning is enhanced through external support and drive.

External support for school improvement

The external change agent has been shown to contribute directly to capacity-building and change. The provision of external support assists schools in moving through different phases of change and improvement. Mitchell and Sackney (2000: 121) suggest that a learning community advances through three learning phases: 'naming and framing, analysing and integrating and applying and experimenting'. These three phases are not mutually exclusive and movement through the phases is a circular and iterative process. Naming and framing involves the establishment of shared understandings; it is the foundation for subsequent development work. During this phase the external change agent (from an LEA, a university or another school) supports the school by facilitating the construction of shared understandings and meanings.

The analysing and integrating phase involves critical reflection and evaluation of current practices. The external change agent assists in this phase by challenging and questioning existing practices. The outcome from this phase is the generation of new ways of doing things and ideas for development. The final phase, applying and experimenting, is where new ideas are put to the test of practice. During this phase the external change agent provides pressure for ideas to be tried out and maintains the momentum for innovation and change.

These three phases broadly reflect the three phases of change outlined by Fullan (1991). Phase 1 is the 'initiation stage' where schools are commencing work and seeking a focus for their improvement work.

Phase 2 is the 'implementation stage' where schools are putting their improvement plans into action. Phase 3 is the 'maintaining and sustaining' phase where the process and practice of school improvement becomes an integral part of school development. At each of these phases, different types of external agency are required to match the particular developmental needs of individual schools.

At the outset, schools will be seeking to establish a developmental focus for their improvement work. While some schools might be very clear about the direction of their improvement efforts, others will need assistance and guidance. The external change agent is well placed to provide such support and is able to assist schools in diagnosing their strengths and weaknesses. This is achieved through the provision of data analysis and critical friendship.

Data analysis and interpretation

Within England and Wales, schools are in receipt of a wide range of data of a comparative nature concerning a school's effectiveness. Often, this data is not presented in a way that is accessible or easily interpreted by schools. Consequently, external change agents can assist schools in understanding and using this data for improvement purposes. The analysis of data by schools is an important means of self-evaluation and can assist schools in focusing upon the most important issues or areas for change.

Critical friendship

Within school improvement, external change agents have an important role to play in offering schools varying degrees of critical friendship. It has been suggested that a critical friend is someone who provides 'a successful marrying of unconditional support and unconditional critique' (MacBeath, 1998: 8). The critical friend requires a particular set of interpersonal and group skills, many of which could be recognised as the province of 'counselling'. Within successful school improvement, these have been found to include reflecting back, reformulating, accepting, challenging and confronting.

Once schools have formulated their improvement plan, they subsequently move into the implementation phase. This requires them to instigate change and to commence their school improvement activities. It is widely acknowledged that during this phase schools require a great deal of support to implement changes successfully. The external change agent, therefore, has an important role to play in providing the practical, technical and emotional support needed by various schools at this critical stage. This support includes staff development and offering evaluative feedback.

Training and staff development

Within any school improvement activity the provision of training and support for staff is essential. External change agents can provide a second tier of training and development opportunities. In many cases, this training is provided in direct response to a particular set of school needs or to address the specific needs of a group of staff within a school.

The external change agent can provide an important source of additional support and training for schools pursuing school improvement. Firstly, external agents can respond quickly to requests for additional support from schools. This 'just in time' in-service training has been shown to be an important component of other highly successful school improvement programmes (Earl and Lee, 1998). Secondly, external change agents have local knowledge of the school and this informs their approach to training. They are therefore more able to match their training style and content to the needs of particular groups of staff. Thirdly, external change agents can offer schools follow-up visits and provide ongoing support that builds upon the training provision.

Evaluative feedback

The importance of enquiry and reflection within the process of school improvement is well established. Within the school improvement cycle evaluation is an important and a necessary means of feedback. The external change agent can provide evaluative feedback to schools that allows them to take stock of progress with their innovation or development work. This collection and use of data to inform development reinforces the centrality of enquiry and reflection within the school's improvement work.

Networking and dissemination

Within school improvement, teacher development is a high priority and teachers are encouraged to build their own professional communities both within and outside the school. External change agents can play a central role in establishing professional networks or communities through their work with schools. They provide additional professional development opportunities and use their local knowledge to establish links between schools for support and developmental purposes. External change agents also have mechanisms for disseminating good practice. They are able to link effective practices across schools and to draw upon good practice from the outside.

The schools that make the most dramatic advances in school improvement have been shown to be those which have used links with other schools to maximum advantage (Harris, 2000b). The networks facilitated by external change agents have been shown to provide schools with important opportunities to learn from each other and to solve problems collectively. These professional communities have been shown to be highly influential in enabling schools to move forward and instrumental in sustaining school improvement.

The work of Miles *et al.* (1988: 23) explains why this form of external support is so important in school improvement. This work offers a categorisation of roles and relationships that describes the ways in which 'outsiders' might facilitate internal development. This list includes:

- diagnosing organisations;
- confidence-building;
- conflict mediation;
- building trust;
- offering support and generating collaboration.

The external change agent has an important part to play in assisting schools with the three phases or stages of school improvement. They offer an important source of pressure and support providing critical friendship when needed. The external change agent cannot instigate or implement change on behalf of the school. They can only facilitate and assist others in managing the process of change. They are there to contribute to building the internal capacity for improvement through their expertise, support and guidance.

Building internal capacity for improvement

The evidence base concerning school improvement highlights the importance of school improvement from 'within' and emphasises the centrality of teachers and students in this endeavour. There is a great deal of support within the literature to suggest that school improvement should be 'owned' by the individual school and its students. Furthermore, it is suggested that there needs to be a focus upon school culture as the main way of understanding the potential for school growth and development. School improvement essentially involves a transformation of the attitudes, beliefs and values that operate within a school. At the core of school improvement is the transformation of a school culture so that it empowers and energises both staff and students.

Teachers

The message that comes across strongly in the literature is that improving schools are ones which have learned to manage multiple change and are moving towards the concept of a learning organisation. But how exactly does this happen? One means of promoting this is to invest in teacher professional development, widely regarded as a key means of promoting school improvement (Joyce, 1990). Reporting on a study of school improvement Gray *et al.* (1999: 144) concluded that a common theme of schools that were improving more rapidly was that 'they had found ways of facilitating more discussion among colleagues about classroom issues than hitherto'.

Joyce *et al.* (1999) argue for a model of school improvement in which the school is a *learning community* for teachers as well as students. This involves teachers feeling able to experiment and take risks, where collaboration is valued and time allocated to facilitate shared work, where information is used as a basis for joint enquiry and where sharing and partnership rather than competition between teachers is encouraged. The term *professional learning community* concerns the establishment of a school-wide culture that:

- emphasises professionalism and is 'client-orientated' and knowledge-based;
- emphasises learning and thus places a high value on teacher professional development;
- emphasises personal connections.

There are also a number of 'preconditions' which appear to enable or facilitate the development of professional learning communities. In the area of *human and social resources*, there is openness to improvement, trust and respect, access to expertise, supportive leadership, and socialisation. In the area of *structural supports*, there are issues of time and places to meet and talk; as well as interdependent teacher roles, communication structures, teacher empowerment and school autonomy. Research also suggests that within professional learning communities students play a significant and important role (Louis, Marks and Kruse, 1995).

Students

School improvement is essentially about constructing a better match between schools and young people. It is essentially about changing schools and, by definition, the patterns of relationships that exist between staff and students. All too often, however, the students' voice is neglected in school improvement work and rarely are students given the opportunity to engage in or inform school improvement efforts. Despite hundreds of studies concerning school improvement there are relatively few that focus attention on the students' contribution to school-level development and change. There is now an emerging evidential base that shows the contribution that student voice can make to school improvement. Writers like Rudduck *et al.* (1996) and Beresford (2000) have reiterated that students have a great deal to say about their experiences of learning and on the whole their voices are constructive and informative.

The contemporary pressures upon teachers make it more difficult to find the space and time to plan and nurture student participation in school. Only too rarely are there opportunities to listen to students' views and accounts of how they learn most effectively. But where such opportunities are made for students to become active participants in the process of improvement and development the gains are significant (Rudduck *et al.* 1996). In schools where students are co-researchers and contribute to the process of change in conjunction with teachers, the potential for improvement is greatly enhanced. It would seem that students have a huge potential contribution to make to school improvement.

It takes time and considerable preparation to build a climate in which both teachers and students feel comfortable working together on issues of school improvement. The boundaries of role have to be crossed and the limits of trust have to be tested. Rudduck (2001: 14) provides four levels of engaging students in the process of school improvement:

1   *Listening to students*: students are a source of data; teachers respond to student data but students are not involved in discussion of data; there is no feedback; teachers act on the data.
2   *Students as active participants*: teachers initiate enquiry and interpret the data but students are taking some role in decision-making.
3   *Students as researchers*: students are involved in enquiry and have an active role in decision-making.
4   *Students as fully active researchers and co-researchers*: students and teachers jointly initiate enquiry; students play an active role in decision-making together with teachers; they jointly plan action in the light of data and review the impact of the intervention.

The student-voice movement is gaining more support among teachers as a means of prompting meaningful innovation and change. There

---

REFLECTION

How far do students participate in improvement activities in your school?
Which of the four levels best reflects students in your school?
How could students be more involved in the process of school improvement?

---

is now increasing interest in developing student consultation and participation. Rudduck (2001: 14) argues that 'constructing a better match between schools and young people entails some fundamental and difficult re-appraisal. Schools will need support, in particular, in the task of re-shaping long standing structures that have fostered disconnection, separateness and division.' If students are to play a more active role in school improvement, then such divisions need to be dismantled and there need to be new structures in place that promote the student voice and allow staff and students to work together collaboratively.

School improvement group

Case studies of schools that are improving demonstrate that they usually involve some form of school improvement group that comprises both staff and students (West *et al.*, 2000). The purpose of this group is to act as a catalyst for change within the school and to generate the internal capacity for change and development. Some consensus about what helps the school improvement group to work successfully is emerging along with evidence about how different groups function in order to bring about change and development. Recent research concerning effective group working highlights that at the start of the school improvement process there is a tension between planning and action (Harris, 2001a). Schools often spend a large amount of time planning for improvement with little emphasis upon action. The school improvement group therefore has an important role to play in generating a bias for action and ensuring that improvement moves from the planning to the implementation stage.

Within any school improvement project a major challenge for schools is to maintain the momentum for innovation and development. There is a tendency for well-intentioned change to be lost at the point of implementation and for improvement efforts to lose momentum over time. A key role for the school improvement group is to monitor the progress of innovation and development within the school and to provide pressure and support where progress seems to be slow.

Certain conditions are necessary for building and maintaining an effective school improvement group. Firstly, there needs to be a shared and clear sense of purpose, a collective view about the direction and nature of change. Secondly, there has to be trust within the group and open communication between individuals. Thirdly, leadership has to be shared and distributed within the group. Leadership will shift from time to time depending upon the problem or issue facing the group. Fourthly, membership of the group will be temporary and fluid. The focus for development will inevitably evolve and change, thus membership of the group must also be flexible. Finally, there must be opportunities within the group for disagreement and challenge. This constructive disagreement is where the energy for innovation resides. Through critical reflection upon current practices, areas for future development and change emerge.

Both external and internal change agents generate the capacity for change by assisting schools in setting developmental priorities and taking appropriate actions. They are catalysts within the developmental process and offer a particular form of leadership. This leadership is essentially a process of constructing knowledge through the interactions of both the external and internal change agents. From this perspective, leadership is about intervention and change; it is not about position or authority. In successful school improvement, leadership is a distributed activity that is premised upon gaining collective knowledge and understanding. It is inclusive rather than exclusive and is essentially concerned with building organisational capacity and capability for improvement. The next chapter considers the relationship between leadership and school improvement.

QUESTIONS FOR FURTHER EXPLORATION

Successful school improvement involves building the capacity for change and development. This emanates from both external and internal agency. In order to enhance your school's capacity to improve consider the following:

(a) Who are the change agents within your school? Are they being fully utilised?
(b) What external support is currently available to your school? How effective is this support?
(c) How far are students involved in your school improvement work? Could they have greater involvement?
(d) How could the school's capacity for improvement be extended? What needs to happen?

5 Leading school improvement

Introduction

The contribution of leadership to school improvement is widely acknowledged and supported in the research literature. Findings from diverse countries draw similar conclusions about the centrality of leadership to school improvement. 'Essentially, schools that improve have leaders that make a significant and measurable contribution to the development of the school and the effectiveness of their staff' (West *et al.*, 2000: 36). Over twenty years ago HMI stated that without exception 'the most single factor in the success of schools is the quality of leadership' (DES, 1977: 36). Since then the school effectiveness and school improvement researchers have reiterated the importance of leadership in schools. 'Leadership helps to establish a clear and consistent vision for the school, which emphasises the prime purposes of the school as teaching and learning and is highly visible to both staff and students' (Sammons *et al.* 1997: 199).

The importance of leadership in securing sustainable school improvement has been demonstrated in both research and practice (Jackson, 2000; Harris and Bennett, 2001). Hallinger and Heck (1996) highlight four areas in which leadership influences school improvement. The first is through establishing and conveying the *purposes* and *goals* of the school. A second area of leadership influence is through the interplay between the *school's organisation* and its *social network*. A third is through *influence over people* and the fourth is in relation to *organisational culture*. Their review of the literature highlights the centrality of the leader in relation to instructional improvement and shows how far leadership influences student and school performance. Hopkins (2001: 114) argues 'that the prime function of leadership for authentic school improvement is to enhance the quality of teaching and learning'. Effective leaders place an emphasis upon teaching and learning as well as building organisational capacity. They have a moral obligation to see that students are well served and that teachers are supported in their efforts to improve the quality of learning. In this sense, leaders must strive to be model learners, to question current practices and to be willing to seek out new findings about their profession.

From a policy-maker's perspective, school leaders are viewed as holding the key to resolving a number of the problems currently facing schools. This has led to a major investment in the preparation and development of school leaders across many countries and has proved pivotal in the establishment of a National College for School Leadership. There has also been an increasing emphasis upon the links between leadership and the culture of the organisation as a route to school improvement. This has encouraged a movement away from the notion of leadership as a series of *transactions* within a given context towards a view of leadership as *transformational*, having the potential to alter the cultural context in which people work. This transformational leadership perspective, as Duignan and Macpherson (1992) explain, focuses on the moral values and value-laden activities of a leader and how these are disclosed to other colleagues. Blase and Anderson (1995) argue that leaders acting in this mode try to use power with or through other people, rather than exercising control over them. Transformational leadership is people- rather than organisation-orientated and requires a leadership approach that transforms the feelings, attitudes and beliefs of others.

There is evidence to demonstrate a positive relationship between transformational leadership approaches and school improvement. This has been shown to involve the building of school cultures or promoting culture behaviours that contribute directly to school improvement (Leithwood *et al.*, 1999). Culture-building by transformational leaders includes behaviours aimed at developing school norms, values, beliefs and assumptions that are student-centred and support continuing professional development. Some of behaviours utilised by transformational leaders to strengthen the school culture include reinforcing with staff, norms of excellence for their own work and the students and assisting staff to clarify shared beliefs and values and to act in accord with such beliefs and values. Transformational leaders provide opportunities for collaboration between staff and are mainly concerned with sharing power with others.

REFLECTION

How far is the leadership in your school transactional, transformational or instructional?
To what extent is leadership shared within the school?

Effective leaders view themselves as the source of a vision for their institutions, working through various processes of consultation, to enlist the support and commitment of staff. In this respect, leadership for school improvement is highly contingent on both context and situation. The choices leaders make will inevitably relate to their own beliefs, values and leadership style. Of central importance in this model of leadership is the cooperation and alignment of others to the leaders' values and vision with those of the leader. Through a variety of symbolic gestures and action, within school improvement leaders are successful at realigning both staff and students to their particular vision of the school.

Leadership and school improvement

There are a number of important findings concerning leadership which offer some relevant insights into the relationship between leadership and improvement. Riley (2000: 47) suggests that

- There is no one package for school leadership, no one model to be learned and applied regardless of culture or context. However leadership can be developed and nurtured.
- School leadership is more than the effort of a single individual.
- School leadership is not static.
- School leaders do not learn how to do leadership. They are often rule breakers and are willing to change in response to new sets of circumstances.

In research on school leaders in Denmark, Scotland, England and Australia, John MacBeath and his colleagues asked teachers to choose from five definitions of leadership which were closest to and furthest away from their views of an effective leader. The core characteristics of effective leaders were as follows:

1 Leadership means having a clear personal vision of what you want to achieve.
2 Good leaders are in the thick of things, working alongside their colleagues.
3 Leadership means respecting teachers' autonomy, protecting them from extraneous demands.
4 Good leaders look ahead, anticipate change and prepare people for it so that it doesn't surprise or dis-empower them.
5 Good leaders are pragmatic. They are able to grasp the realities of the political and economic context and they are able to negotiate and compromise.
6 Good leaders are informed by and communicate clear sets of personal and educational values which represent their moral purposes for the school (Macbeath, 1998: 63).

The evidence from the international literature demonstrates that effective leaders exercise an indirect but powerful influence on the effectiveness of the school and on the achievement of students. It shows that effective school leaders exercise both professional and political leadership and are able to draw on their past experience to respond to new situations. Leadership for school improvement falls into a number of phases. West *et al.* (2000: 32) have clarified these phases as follows:

• Initial interest in the personal qualities and characteristics of 'successful leaders' which result in *personality or trait* theories of leadership;
• Increasing focus on what it is that leaders actually do – are there some behaviours and approaches that are consistently associated with successful leadership? Such inquiries support the development of *behavioural theories* of leadership;
• Growing awareness that task related and people centred behaviours may be interpreted quite differently by different groups and in

different contexts, prompting explanation of how the particular context might be best accounted for within a general theory, and resulting in a variety of *situational approaches* to leadership;

• Most recently, emphasis upon the links between leadership style and the culture of the organisation – a notion of leadership as *transformational* – having the potential to alter the context in which people work.

This last phase has been at the forefront of much research and writing in the past decade. The debate between transactional and transformational leadership has dominated both policy and practice in a number of different countries. Transactional leadership consists of doing something, for, to and on behalf of others. It is also premised upon tasks being delegated to followers and the followers completing these tasks. This form of leadership is one that emphasises procedures and hard data to inform decision-making. Based upon an exchange of services for various kinds of rewards that the leader controls, the role of the transactional leader is to focus upon the purposes of the organisation and to assist people to recognise what needs to be done in order to reach a desired outcome. In countries where the systems of command and control are in place there has been an interest in and focus upon transactional leadership.

Alternatively, in countries where decentralisation has occurred, there has been renewed interest in transformational leadership and more democratic leadership approaches. This style of leadership is people- rather than organisation-orientated and requires a leadership approach that transforms the feelings, attitudes and beliefs of others. In other words, it transforms 'school culture' which is the main aim of school improvement. In this sense, transformational leadership is the style that offers the most promise for school improvement. This type of leadership is more concerned with securing collaboration amongst staff than getting particular tasks performed.

Within school improvement the quality of leadership is a key factor in building a school community where improvement is most likely to occur. Effective leaders not only have a vision for their school but also recognise the importance of staff working together to achieve this vision. In order for school improvement to occur school leaders need to know the strengths and weaknesses of staff and need to invest in their growth and development. In the current climate of rapid change, the task facing school leaders is much more complex and diverse. Leaders therefore must become more sophisticated in their ability to manage change and in sustaining a culture of opportunity for students and teachers. However, this cannot be achieved in isolation but depends upon teachers and students who trust one another and work together with a common purpose. It depends upon building a school community that is inclusive and values, above all, individual development and achievement.

Current perspectives on leadership

The various demands and challenges facing those leading schools in the current context have been outlined in recent study into effective headship in the UK (Harris *et al.*, 2001). The two most important aspects of this form of leadership are firstly, that effective leaders are constantly and consistently managing several competing tensions and dilemmas; and, secondly, effective leaders are, above all, people-centred.

> Managers know that people make the critical difference between success and failure. The effectiveness with which organisations manage, develop, motivate, involve and engage the willing contribution of the people who work in them is a key determinant of how well those organisations perform . . . employee commitment and positive 'psychological contact' between employer and employee are fundamental to improving performance.
>
> (Patterson *et al.*, 1997: vii–viii)

This form of leadership starts not from the basis of power and control but from the ability to act with others and to enable others to act. Effective leaders must have the ability to read and adjust to the particular context or set of circumstances they face. In this respect, their leadership behaviour is contingent on context and situation. The choices that they make relate directly to their own beliefs, values and leadership style (Harris and Chapman, 2002).

In the current climate, the capacity of leaders to make a difference depends upon their interpretation of and responses to the constraints, demands and choices that they face. Effective leaders must know how to span boundaries in order to promote information and to generate the capacity for improvement. At the same time as they negotiate the constraints of internal and external environments, they must capitalise on the many opportunities for making choices.

Centrally important in leadership for school improvement is the cooperation and alignment of others to the leaders' values and vision. As Bhindi and Duigan (1996) suggest:

> Authentic leaders breathe the life force into the workplace and keep the people feeling energised and focused. As stewards and guides they build people and their self esteeem. They derive their credibility from personal integrity and 'walking' their values.
>
> (1996: 29)

Leadership for school improvement reflects what has been termed by Stoll and Fink (1996) as 'invitational leadership'. Effective leaders tend to be reflective, caring and highly principled people who emphasise the human dimension of the management enterprise. They place a high premium upon personal values and are more concerned with cultural rather than structural change.

West *et al.* (2000: 38) draw three conclusions about leadership in schools that are improving:

* School leaders in these schools develop expanded repertoires of leadership;
* Such schools offer a context for the development of new understandings about leadership style;
* In such schools collaborative enquiry provides the opportunity for teachers to study, to learn about and to share leadership.

In short, effective school leaders build the capacity for improvement within their schools. They generate the conditions and create the climate for improvement to be initiated and sustained. Effective leaders orchestrate rather than dictate improvement.

Leading improvement

In schools that are improving a distinctive feature is how far they work as a *learning community*. Within improving schools, a climate of collaboration exists and there is a collective commitment to work together. This climate is not simply given but is the result of discussion, development and dialogue amongst those working within the organisation. An 'improving' community consists of teachers who are active in constructing meaning and collaborating in mutual enquiry and learning. An improving community is also a learning community where the learning of teachers receives the same attention as the learning of students. As Mitchell and Sackney note:

> We believe that teachers need the same kind of conditions in the staff room to teach well that students need in the classroom to learn. It is one of the most devastating ironies of education that teachers are expected to provide a safe learning environment for their students within a teaching environment that is anything but safe for the teachers.
>
> (2000: 9)

The role of the leader in school improvement is to ensure that the school is a learning environment for both staff and students. This necessarily involves building the capacity within the school for learning and improvement to take place. Successful leaders promote the climate for improvement in their school in a number of important ways.

Consistent vision and values

In order for school improvement to take place leaders need to create a balance between a sense of vision and capacity-building among staff. The articulation, development and implementation of 'vision' is particularly important in capacity-building for improvement.

> It is one thing for a leader to have the vision: it is quite another for that vision to guide the behaviour of an entire organisation. Leaders in successful quality settings have been able to conceptualise the theory in ways that translate into practice, steer the change process, and guide their people in determining not only how to perform their jobs, but even more importantly, what those jobs should be.
>
> (Day *et al.*, 2000: 20)

A leader's vision can have a powerful impact upon the culture of a school and can provide the direction for school-level change and development. A recent study of effective leadership by Day *et al.* (2000) found that the practice of good leadership is underpinned by a number of core *personal values*. These concerned the modelling and promotion of respect (for individuals), fairness and equality, caring for the well-being and whole development of students and staff, integrity and honesty. In addition effective leaders have a determination that all students and teachers achieve high standards through a combination of high expectations and team work. This means that they place a continuing pressure on self and others for improvement.

Maximising staff potential

Effective leaders promote staff development and invest in the development of their staff. It is important that this development not only focuses upon needs of direct benefit to the school and classroom but those of direct benefit to the individual. The leaders' emphasis on the continuing development of staff shows a clear recognition that the teachers are their most important asset in the pursuit of classroom and school improvement. High expectations and a determination to achieve the highest possible standards sometimes mean pushing staff to the limit.

Creating a learning organisation

Schools have often been described as dynamic learning systems. The school-improvement literature highlights two themes that have relevance to the school as a learning organisation. The first concerns professional development and the need to create opportunities for teachers not only to work together but also to learn together. A systematic and integrated approach to staff development that focuses on the professional learning of teachers and establishes the classroom as an important centre for teacher development is central to successful school improvement. Evidence suggests that staff development is the central strategy for supporting teachers as they engage in improvement activities. Attention to teacher learning has direct spin-offs in terms of student learning. Where teachers expand and develop their own teaching repertoires, it is more likely that they will provide an increased range of learning opportunities for students. Fortunately, schools are well placed to develop the human and intellectual capital, so the second issue relates to the forms of professional development that teachers encounter.

Fullan (1991) provides a bleak picture of in-service initiatives that are poorly conceptualised, insensitive to the concerns of individual participants and, perhaps critically, make little effort to help participants relate their learning experiences to their usual workplace conditions. The effectiveness of staff development initiatives to change or influence classroom practice is far from encouraging. In order to achieve improvements in teaching and better learning outcomes for students, teachers need to be engaged in professional development that promotes creativity and innovation. Using peer coaching, mentoring and off-site visits rather than the conventional in-service training format has been shown to have positively affected teaching and learning outcomes.

Working with others

The most important aspect of building improvement capacity is working successfully with people. Effective leaders display a whole range of interpersonal qualities – empathy, trust, credibility, courage, honesty, fairness.

> It's enabling other people . . . to take over, to do things . . . It's being able to trust other people. To be confident in your own ability . . . to delegate tasks and know they will be done . . . to allow people to do things and not to try and control it all
>
> (Day *et al.*, 2000: 16)

By definition good leaders are not only enthusiastic about their jobs and the potential and achievements of the organisation in which they work, they are also believers in their own judgement. They are ruthless in their establishment of high expectations, aware of the need to think strategically, willing to take risks to do so – though these will be based upon an intimate knowledge of their own constituency.

In summary, effective leadership for school improvement involves leaders:

- being clear in their vision for the school and communicating this to others;
- creating, maintaining and constantly monitoring relationships;
- being prepared to take risks in order to achieve goals;
- building capacity both inside and outside the school;
- managing ongoing tensions and dilemmas.

Effective leadership for school improvement is a form of collaborative leadership where a number of strategies are used for bringing out the best in staff. These strategies include:

- the power of praise;
- involving others in decision-making;
- giving professional autonomy;
- leading by standing behind, alongside and in front.

The overarching message about effective leadership for school improvement is one of building the community of the school in its widest sense, i.e. through developing and involving others. Effective leadership for school improvement is about capacity-building in others, it is people-centred and premised upon personal and professional values. It suggests a model of leadership that is premised upon continuous change and is transformational.

However, West *et al.* (2000) suggest that there are two particular problems with the transformational leadership approach. The first problem concerns the sustainability of transformational leadership approaches over time. They suggest that 'transformational character-istics are, in our experience, unsustainable over the long haul (West *et al.*, 2000: 39). The second problem relates to the availability of high-quality headteachers who are transformational in their leadership approaches.

This inevitably points towards developing and securing leadership *at other levels* within the organisation to provide leadership that can continuously improve the school. Research evidence concerning school improvement underlines the importance of devolved leadership at different levels within the organisation (Hopkins *et al.*, 1994; Hopkins *et al.*, 1997; Fullan, 1992). The importance of school level, department level and classroom level change has been shown to be essential in successful school improvement programmes (e.g. Hopkins *et al.*, 1996; Harris, 2001a).

REFLECTION

Where is leadership located in your school?
Who are the most effective leaders and what form of leadership do they demonstrate?

Research has shown that a substantial proportion of the variation in effectiveness among schools is due to variation within schools. This work has emphasised the importance of exploring differential effectiveness particularly at the level of the department (Creemers, 1994; Scheerens, 1992; Sammons *et al.* 1996a and b; Harris, *et al.* 1996; Harris, 1998). In particular, the leadership role at the departmental level has been shown to be an important 'missing link' in school improvement (Harris, 2001a). There are increasing calls for and acceptance of the importance of various forms of teacher leadership in securing and sustaining school improvement.

Teacher leadership

A recent reassessment of the leadership role of the headteacher implies that giving others responsibility and developing others is the best possible way of the organisation moving forward. This means relinquishing the idea of structure as control and viewing structure as the vehicle for empowering others. This would suggest that, if school improvement is to be achieved, the emphasis should be upon transformational rather than transactional leadership. Consequently, there are increasing calls for and acceptance of a leadership role for teachers in achieving goals in the context of their own areas of direct responsibility.

Studies of school change have paid little attention to the role of those other than the designated leader in school improvement. The literature propagates a view of leadership that is centred upon strong headteachers with a singular and clear vision for the school. These leaders have dynamic and outgoing personalities with high levels of commitment to their role. In terms of school improvement, transformational leadership is the model of practice that dominates much of the writing. This approach is premised upon leadership being equated with cultural change. Although schools need to be led by individuals who do make a difference, leadership has to be replicated right through the organisation and found in every aspect of school life.

This implies a model of leadership 'where leadership and leader are not the same' (Lambert, 1998: 8). Leadership is a shared and collective endeavour that engages all members of the organisation. It means the context in which people work together and learn together, where they construct and refine meaning leading to a shared purpose or set of goals. This model of leadership implies a redistribution of power and a realignment of authority within the organisation.

There is shared understanding and shared purpose at the core of teacher leadership. It engages all those within the organisation in a reciprocal learning process that leads to collective action and meaningful change. Teacher leadership is premised upon the belief that leadership potential is widely spread amongst organisational members. As West *et al.* point out:

> If this leadership potential is to be realised, then it will have to be grounded in a commitment to learn and develop that inhabits the structures of schools as well as the classroom – it is likely that the school will conceive and act differently from the traditional explanations of leadership and structure. This view of leadership, then is not hierarchical, but federal. It is a view which is both tight and loose; tight on values, but loose on the freedom to act, opportunity to experiment and authority to question historical assumptions.
>
> (2000: 39)

For teacher leadership to be maximised there have to be shared values and goals along with the ability to take action. This can only be achieved as part of a democratic process where individual ideas and actions can be freely expressed. When a school operates democratically then teachers will be more likely to contribute to its development in a positive way.

Although further research concerning the role of teacher leadership within school improvement is needed, there are some tentative conclusions that can be reached. It is suggested that there are four discernible and discrete dimensions of the teacher leadership role within school improvement. The first dimension concerns the way in which teachers help translate the principles of school improvement into the practices of individual classrooms. The limitations of 'top-down' change to impact upon the classroom level are well known. Hence, the importance of teacher leadership is in taking the suggested change or development and implementing it at the classroom level.

Through working with colleagues, teacher leaders can negotiate ways in which the proposed change or development can be directly linked to teaching and learning. This *brokering role* remains a central responsibility for the teacher leader. It ensures that links between whole-school level and classroom level are in place and that opportunities for meaningful development among teachers are enhanced.

A second dimension of the teacher leader role focuses upon empowering teachers and giving them some ownership of a particular change or development. An emphasis is placed upon participative leadership where all teachers feel part of the change or development. Teacher leaders assist other teachers to cohere around a particular development and to foster a more collaborative way of working. They work with colleagues to shape school improvement efforts and take a *guiding role* by encouraging teachers towards a collective goal.

A third dimension of the teacher leadership role in school improvement is a *mediating role*. Teacher leaders are important sources of expertise and information. They are able to draw upon additional resources and expertise if required and to seek external assistance. Finally, a fourth and possibly most important dimension of the teacher leadership role is an *affiliation role*. This requires the forging of close relationships with teachers in order that mutual learning can take place. The way in which teachers learn together has been shown to be an important determinant of school improvement. Lambert's (1998) research found that professional development and learning were distinguishing characteristics of schools that were improving. Lambert (1998: 4) noted that: 'Intense interest in professional development was viewed as an ongoing success for every teacher in the school, as well as for the principal . . . such schools worked to build the capacity of the entire staff to help manage the school . . . and to develop a common knowledge base among all members.'

At a macro-level this might involve monitoring attainment, assessing performance and setting clear targets. At the micro-level it suggests an important coaching or mentoring role for teacher leaders as they work with others on issues of teaching and learning.

Current research has examined how school and teacher leadership affect levels of student engagement. This work explored the effects of school and teacher leadership on students' engagement with school (Leithwood and Jantzi, 2000). The study considered principal and teacher leadership separately, as well as the relative effects of these two sources of leadership. One of the main findings from this study was that the 'effects on student engagement of both sources of leadership are substantially moderated by family educational culture' (Leithwood and Jantzi, 2000: 59). However, the research also found 'that the relationships between principal and teacher leadership are moderately strong explaining 66 per cent of the variation in school conditions, a proportion that does not change by adding family educational culture to the analyses' (Leithwood and Jantzi, 2000: 59).

The findings suggest that both principal and teacher leadership are mediated by most of the same school and classroom conditions; however, teacher leadership explained *more* variation in student learning. The research study concluded that 'teacher leadership far outweighs principal leadership effects before taking into account the moderating effects of family educational culture' (Leithwood and Jantzi, 2000: 60). Evidence from this study suggests that principal leadership does not stand out as a critical part of the change process but that teacher leadership demonstrates a significant effect on student engagement. While the study does not support widely distributed forms of leadership, it does 'support the distribution of a larger proportion of current leadership development resources to the development of teacher leadership' (Leithwood and Jantzi, 2000: 61).

Teacher leaders are able to lead within and beyond the classroom. They identify with and contribute to a community of teacher-learners and leaders who influence others toward improved educational practice. Teachers can be leaders beyond the classroom by

- accepting responsibility for helping colleagues to achieve success for all students in their subject area;
- seeing their role as a developer of other teachers;

- taking the opportunity to influence the quality of classroom practice;
- observing and mentoring others towards improved performance;
- generating discussion about teaching and learning.

Schools improve when individual teachers change their behaviour, attitudes and beliefs. Such changes cannot be imposed but are fostered through collaboration, mentoring and meaningful debate among teachers about classroom practice. Developing teacher leadership inevitably means investing in professional development and training. It also means focusing attention more closely upon the classroom level rather than the school level. If classrooms are to improve, then it requires teachers to have a better understanding of how learning and teaching can be most effective. The next chapter focuses upon classroom improvement.

QUESTIONS FOR FURTHER EXPLORATION

Within schools that are improving leadership is dispersed and distributed to teachers. In order to build the capacity for improvement, teachers are leaders both within and beyond the classroom.

(a) In your school how far do teachers view themselves as leaders?

(b) Are there opportunities for teachers to collaborate, discuss and network?

(c) Is there time set aside for teachers to reflect on their practice with colleagues?

6 Improving classrooms

Introduction

At the centre of school improvement is a concern to improve the quality of teaching and learning in classrooms. Many studies of effective schooling have indicated that the quality of the teacher–student relationship is at the heart of the learning process. Research has shown that improving schools place an emphasis upon the teaching and learning processes and invest in teacher-development time. Indeed, many studies show that factors at classroom level are crucially important in generating and sustaining school improvement. Of all the 'school level characteristics, it is those that relate to teaching that have the most empirical support' (Scheerens, 1992: 17). Furthermore, many of the classroom factors related to school improvement are concerned with the process and practice of effective teaching.

The classroom is the dominant place where learning and teaching take place but, until recently, a common response to the challenge of improving schools has been to mobilise change efforts at the level of the whole school. This type of intervention is premised upon a view that the key to school improvement lies in systems and has led schools to focus their energies upon infra-structural change. While attempts have been made to generate theories of school improvement that reflect the complexity of organisational change, the classroom as a 'unit of analysis' rarely features (Harris, 2001a).

Some researchers within the school-effectiveness and the school improvement research fields have questioned whether the school is the appropriate unit of analysis (Harris and Bennett, 2001). These arguments suggest that to analyse student achievement school by school is to overlook much closer influences on individual student performance. It also suggests that the school is not the only unit of analysis for 'improvement' activities but that other levels or units within the school organisation also need to be considered (Harris, 2001a).

There is a growing recognition that attempts to bring about school improvement will have limited impact in raising student performance and achievement unless a multi-level approach to development is adopted that encompasses school, department and classroom level. It has been estimated that 40 per cent of the variation in achievement can be explained by looking at differences at the classroom level. Similarly, research has identified 'the classroom level as more important for learning outcomes than other levels in education' (Creemers, 1994: 5). While it cannot be denied that there are conditions at the school level which can make classroom improvement more possible, the quality of the teaching and learning process remains the main determinant of educational outcomes (Creemers, 1994).

Classroom improvement

To shift the improvement focus to the classroom level requires investing in developmental approaches that make the maximum impact on student and teacher learning. It also necessitates facilitating the 'deep learning' of teachers through building communities that foster collaboration and professional growth. It is only by focusing attention upon improving teaching and learning that it is possible to generate improvement that impacts directly on student learning and achievement. Improving schools enhance the quality of learning by involving students centrally in the learning process and ensuring that they feel empowered to learn. Teachers build learning capacity within their classrooms when

- students are involved in the learning process by providing a variety of tasks which deal with individual, small-group and large-group situations;
- students work together as part of a team sharing experiences, being given different roles and developing their own self-esteem;
- students are actively involved in a review and reflection of the learning process;

- students use formative and motivational forms of assessment which reinforce learning.

Effective teachers engage students in the process of assisting learners to 'learn how to learn'. This is called 'meta-cognition'. At the core of effective teaching is the arrangement of a learning environment within the classroom that allows students to interact and to 'learn how to learn'. Effective teachers teach their students *how to learn* and thus teaching becomes more productive as students are helped to become more effective learners. As Joyce and Showers note:

> Effective learners draw information, ideas, and wisdom from their teachers and use learning resources effectively. Thus a major role in teaching is to create powerful learners. The same principle applies to schools. Outstanding schools teach their students ways of learning. Thus, teaching becomes more effective as the students progress through those schools because, year by year, the students have been taught to be stronger learners.
>
> (1988: 10)

It is clear that meta-cognitive skills are of great importance in developing problem-solving skills and developing thinking skills generally. Lack of meta-cognitive skills can lead to students using inappropriate problem-solving techniques or adopting ineffective approaches to learning. Muijs and Reynolds (2001: 84) suggest that there are a number of techniques to teach students meta-cognitive strategies:

1 Develop an awareness of thinking processes among students by explaining why problem-solving strategies are important. Demonstrating how problem solving takes place will improve students' understanding of the processes associated with solving problems.
2 Work problems through and present the whole problem resolution not just the final solution. This will allow students the opportunity to follow the patterns of problem solving.
3 Let the class as a whole work through a problem, with the teacher providing feedback, help and guidance to assist the class to solve the problem.

Refining meta-cognitive skills can also be assisted through specific teaching approaches or activities. For example, cooperative group work and inductive teaching have both been shown to enhance meta-cognitive skills and abilities (Hopkins and Harris, 2000). Both these models of teaching allow students to practise information-processing and scaffolding techniques. A major challenge for all teachers is to consider the best way to foster and develop students' ability to 'learn how to learn' and to maximise their learning potential and capability. This will inevitably mean drawing upon learning theory and research findings concerning effective learning.

How students learn

To date a vast number of psychological concepts, principles and processes have been identified as underlying aspects of effective learning. The emphasis given to different psychological concepts, principles and processes differs across the various theories and frameworks employed as a basis for instructional psychology. However, it is possible to identify four different traditions of learning theory that arose from very different beginnings: cognitive theory, behavioural theory, social and personality theory and humanistic theory.

Cognitive learning

Cognitive learning theories grew out of experimental interest in the ways adults remembered lists of words or syllables. Cognitive theories cover the domain of words, logic language, reasoning and knowledge. Piaget argued that in order to understand how children think one has to look at the qualitative development of their ability to solve problems. Cognitive development in this sense is more than the addition of new facts or ideas but is the ability to address problems in a more sophisticated way. The role of the teacher therefore is that of *problem-setter* by presenting a range of facts and arguments. Cognitive theories address complex forms of learning like problem-solving and understanding language.

Behavioural theories

Behavioural theories were developed by psychologists such as Pavlov and Skinner from the 1920s onwards to predict and explain the behaviour of animals in certain learning situations, i.e. learning to press a lever to get food, or to recognise and respond to a new signal for food. Behavioural theorists concentrate on directly observable behaviour and the theory is connected to teaching in small steps, with practice and review, a model used in direct instruction. These stimuli–response studies became known as conditioning models and were extended to more general concerns like the development of physical skills and the role of reward and punishment in the education of children. With behavioural theory the important thing is drill, practice and repetition. The teacher is seen as a *trainer and provider* of rewards and punishments.

Social and personality theory development

This started in the 1940s with a desire to account for the differences between individuals in the ways they learn and make sense of the world. Subsequent decades saw the growth of a wider study of the role of society in the formation of personality, the nature of the sense of self and the more general and profound issues linking the individual to the social world. Social and personal theories largely focus upon attitudes, beliefs, opinions and judgements about the self and others. Here the teacher is a *facilitator* of learning.

Humanistic learning theories

These originated from the attempt to explain how people's feelings and their capacity to feel were changed by various sorts of group, or one-to-one counselling experiences. These theories focused upon concepts such as love, vulnerability, acceptance, etc., and it is only within this tradition that the role of awareness in learning has been studied. In humanistic learning the focus is upon teacher as *counsellor* rather than teacher as trainer. Within this theory, the emphasis is upon the teacher managing and organising the right conditions so that effective learning can take place.

REFLECTION

What are the implications of these four theories of learning for classroom practice?
How far do they imply different types of classroom activities and experiences?

Whichever learning theory is adopted or favoured by teachers, as Kyriacou (1986) pointed out, there are three crucial aspects of effective learning:

- the student must be attending to the learning experience;
- the student must be receptive to the learning experience;
- the learning must be appropriate for the desired learning to take place.

These three aspects form the basis of the general conditions required for learning to take place. The effectiveness of a teacher's classroom activity is dependent upon an understanding of the way those principles interact with practical teaching.

To learn most effectively students need to be 'effective gatherers, organisers and expressers of knowledge' (Kyriacou, 1986: 32). In any group of students there are wide differences in aptitudes, abilities and background knowledge. These 'individual differences' and their interactions with learning settings have been the focus of a great deal of research activity. It has been shown that some differences are more proximal to the practice of learning than others. The theories and beliefs that students hold about knowledge and learning have a significant influence upon their approach to learning. Some students will take a 'deep approach' to learning and will seek active engagement with the content and seek understanding. Other students will take a 'surface approach' and are preoccupied with memorising the content.

REFLECTION

In your school, how prevalent are surface and deep learning?
What are the classroom practices that lead to deep learning?

It is generally agreed that to become an effective learner requires
adopting a 'deep approach' to learning where higher levels of understanding and meta-cognition are sought. This will require the learner to
learn about the process of learning, to set specific learning goals and
to seek feedback upon progress towards these goals. Much of the advice
teachers give to learners rarely focuses upon the process of learning
itself. Teaching students how to learn necessitates that teachers have an
understanding of the key components of effective learning.

Effective learning

The literature shows that effective learning always involves a modification of what the learner already knows or believes. What students are
doing as they learn can be understood only in terms of the way their
previous experience has set them up to construe the new situation.
Learning, therefore, can be guided and assisted successfully only in the
light of this understanding. In acquiring knowledge successful learners
are always actively involved with the teacher and the topic. They are
engaged with the learning and actively seek ways of connecting together
the various components of learning.

Making links

The essence of effective learning lies in the ability to relate what learners
already know to new learning. If what is taught does not engage with
the learner's previous understanding it will be ignored and learning will
be ineffective. Consequently, effective teaching must take into account
the implicit theories which learners hold already. These implicit theories
can direct learners' attention and can channel their thoughts. These
theories are often very stable and resistant to change. They can derive
from first-hand experience, informal social interaction and formal

tuition or teaching. It is important, therefore, that these implicit theories are made explicit in order for learning to take place.

High expectations

An important part of effective learning is the extent to which students feel that they are expected to learn and how this expectation of learning is reinforced. One of the most important factors both in classroom climate and in school and teacher effectiveness are the teacher's expectations of students. Students that teachers expect to do well will tend to achieve more, while conversely students who are expected to do badly fulfil their teachers' expectations as well. Negative expectations can be a particular problem in schools in disadvantaged areas. In these schools, low expectations can become endemic and contribute to consistent under-performance. Thus, a central task must be to ensure that all teachers hold high expectations of students irrespective of socio-economic context.

The issue for teachers is how to alter negative expectation effects? Muijs and Reynolds (2001: 65) provide a very useful checklist of suggestions of ways to overcome this problem:

- Remember that all students can learn and communicate that belief to students.
- Make sure that all students get the opportunity to participate in classroom activities such as questioning and discussion.
- Be aware of potential differences in your response to students.
- Monitor how you distribute rewards and punishments.

The expectations a teacher holds can affect students in a variety of ways. Consequently, by being vigilant about the nature and type of communication that occurs within a classroom teachers are more likely to reduce the effects of negative expectations upon student performance and achievement.

Learning in context

Research has emphasised that effective learning is 'context-dependent'. It has been shown that locating and embedding learning within a specified context enhances learning. While some features of effective learning are generic and apply across all contexts – e.g. high expectations – there are certain contexts where specific learning features apply. For example, in a class where students are engaging in cooperative learning, it may be necessary to teach the rules of cooperation, i.e. listening, sharing, helping each other, before engaging students in cooperative learning activities. In different socio-economic contexts, teaching practices may also vary to suit the learning needs of the different groups. Muijs and Reynolds (2001: 213) give the following summary of teacher behaviours that are necessary to secure attainment in low-economic status contexts:

- generating a warm and supportive affect by letting children know help is available;
- getting a response, any response, before moving on to the next bit of material;
- presenting material in small bits, with a chance to practise before moving on;
- showing how bits fit together before moving on;
- emphasising knowledge and applications before abstraction, putting the concrete first;
- giving immediate help;
- generating strong structure;
- using individually differentiated material;
- using the experiences of students.

Muijs and Reynolds (2001: 214) also note that within middle socio-economic status contexts the teaching behaviours differ to include:

- requiring extended reasoning;
- posing questions that require associations and generalisations;
- giving difficult material;
- using projects that require independent judgement, discovery and problem solving;
- encouraging learners to take responsibility for their own learning;
- rich verbalising.

Context influences the process of learning but should not restrict learning. Effective learning is an active process in which students draw upon contextual factors to help them to create meaning and to articulate understanding. One thing that distinguishes successful from unsuccessful learners is the ability to recognise and articulate what it is they do not know, or do not understand. The skill of being articulate about intellectual knowledge is an important strategy for amplifying that knowledge.

Motivation

Whether intrinsic or extrinsic, motivation is a vital factor in effective learning as it is closely related to self-concept and to personal needs. Praise, recognition and approval from the teacher can help satisfy needs for acceptance and are also basic to feelings of self-esteem. Intrinsic motivation occurs in situations in which the motivation for learning comes entirely from the task to be performed. The student learns because of the interest in the topic or activity, or in order to find an answer to a puzzling question or a solution to a pressing problem. Extrinsic motivation comes from the portrayal of the subject as being important, interesting and rewarding.

Differentiating learning

Recognising and accommodating individual differences amongst learners is an important component of effective teaching and effective learning. Its underlines the need for learners to believe in themselves as learners and to accept that they may have a preferred way of learning (Wood, 1988). The stronger students' feelings of self-efficacy the higher the level of achievement. Consequently, teachers need to reward, praise and respect students as a means to improving students' self-esteem and improving their achievement.

Locus of control

Research has shown that achievement can be judged by learners in either internal or external ways. If achievement is judged by learners in terms of internal factors such as lack of ability or lack of effort the result is de-motivation and a reluctance to learn. Alternatively, if achievement is judged in external ways such as poor teaching or scarcity of books, the effect on motivation is less damaging. In this case failure is ascribed to external factors and does not damage a student's motivation to learn because it is viewed as not 'their fault'.

Dweck and Repucci (1973) argue that girls and boys attribute failure to quite different causes – girls to lack of ability (internal) and boys to their lack of effort (internal) or bad luck (external) – and that their teachers, often unwittingly, provide differential feedback to them. The net result of this is that learners are less likely to do well if the reinforcement obtained from the teacher focuses on internal causes. To increase motivation teachers need to move away from internal causes and to raise expectations through focusing on positive achievement and learning gain.

Opportunities to learn

The opportunity to learn is an important variable in explaining variations between schools and teachers. An important part of effective teaching is the extent to which learners feel that they are expected to learn and how opportunities to learn are provided. The importance of individual differences amongst learners underlines the need for learners to believe in themselves as learners. A relatively new strand of work on learning theory concerns what is known as 'self-efficacy'. In this theory the learners' beliefs in themselves are reinforced or reduced and the effects on achievement noted. The research shows that the stronger their feeling of self-efficacy the better the level of achievement. Moreover, the individual's feeling is influenced by the school attended. If teachers hold positive views about ability and about their teaching skills they are more likely to produce academic learning in their classrooms.

The school improvement literature has consistently shown the importance of the classroom environment on learning and students' motivation to learn. It highlights how the teacher influences the learning environment of the classroom. As Kyriacou (1991: 13) points out, effective teaching is primarily concerned 'with setting up a learning activity, task or experience for each student which is successful in bringing about the type of student learning (knowledge, understanding, skills and attitudes) the teacher intends'.

The key to being an effective teacher lies in knowing what to do to generate students' learning and achievement. To this end there have been numerous theories of teaching approaches or styles. However, the effective teacher does not necessarily fit neatly into such categories or typologies. Whatever the relative merits of different teaching approaches or styles the research findings still reveal little concrete evidence in favour of one approach rather than another. In terms of enhancing teacher effectiveness in the classroom it would appear that a mixture of approaches or methods is preferable. Indeed research evidence concerning classroom improvement is highly consistent in the features or characteristics associated with effective teaching.

Effective teaching

A number of writers have attempted to identify the key aspects of effective teaching and have focused upon the psychological aspects of instruction such as the effects of reinforcement on learning. Other writers on this theme have focused upon general qualities (or teaching skills) which seem to be of importance such as planning and lesson-pacing. Such studies point towards the importance of utilising classroom time to the maximum to guarantee effective teaching. Classroom studies of teaching effects have generally supported a direct and structured approach to teaching. The school-effectiveness research movement has similarly endorsed the importance of direct or structured teaching. The literature is consistent over the fact that effective teachers:

- begin lessons with a review of relevant previous material and a preview of what is to be learned;
- present material in small steps with clear and detailed explanations and active student practice after each step;
- guide students in initial practice by asking questions and checking for understanding;

- provide systematic feedback and corrections;
- supervise independent practice;
- provide regular testing and review (Creemers, 1994: 5).

Effective teachers structure the content by beginning with an overview, outlining objectives, calling attention to the main ideas, summarising sub-parts as the lesson progresses and reviewing main ideas at the end. They then guide learners and provide concept maps or summaries to make explicit the connection between the various parts. Effective teachers reinforce learning by repeating and reviewing general rules and concepts. They present clearly, enthusiastically and pace accordingly.

Effective teaching involves creating a learning environment which:

- emphasises learning goals and makes them explicit;
- outlines learning purposes and potential learning outcomes;
- carefully organises and sequences curriculum experiences;
- explains and illustrates what students are to learn;
- frequently asks direct and specific questions to monitor students' progress and check their understanding;
- provides students with ample opportunity to practise, gives prompts and feedback to ensure success and corrects errors;
- reviews regularly and holds students accountable for work.

Source: Harris and Hopkins (2000)

From this perspective a teacher promotes learning by being active in planning and organising instruction, explaining to students what they are to learn, arranging occasions for guided practice, monitoring progress, providing feedback and otherwise helping students to understand and accomplish work. In this role the teacher is the leader and presenter of learning and demonstrates personal attributes, technical competencies and subject knowledge that will promote students' learning in an atmosphere of respect and confidence.

Teachers are most effective in teaching basic skills, when they:

- structure learning experiences;
- proceed in small steps but at a brisk pace;
- give detailed and redundant instructions, explanations and examples;
- ask a large number of questions and provide overt student practice;
- provide feedback and corrections, especially in the initial stages of learning new material;
- have a student success rate of 80 per cent or higher, especially in initial learning;
- divide assignments into smaller assignments and find ways to control frequently;
- provide for continued student practice; students may even learn more than is necessary; they may have a success rate of 90–100 per cent and become rapid, firm and self-confident (Rosenshine, 1983).

The research literature has consistently shown that maximisation of teaching time is an important construct of effective teaching and learning (Creemers, 1994). Attentiveness of classes can vary from below 50 per cent of the time to as high as 90 per cent. It would appear, therefore, that student engaged time is an important concept when considering effective teaching. The achievement of learners has been shown to be heavily influenced by the way time is allocated by teachers and used by learners in classrooms (Kyriacou, 1986). It follows that interventions which affect instructional time or active learning time will affect achievement. In other words, not only is the amount of time students spend 'on task' essential for effective teaching, but also the nature of the task is important for effective learning to take place.

Other studies highlighted the tensions that exist between attempts to maximise student engagement and attempts to maximise success rate. Engagement is generally higher during activities conducted by the teacher than during independent student work. Through careful differentiation programmes, however, such difficulties can be overcome and students can learn as effectively in groups and independently. Some studies have thus sought to employ a notion of *active learning time* that focuses on the nature of each student's active mental engagement in the learning activities. In essence this development attempts to move away from a notion of students being occupied to a view of students having an appropriate mental engagement with the task.

Another important aspect of effective teaching time is ensuring that the students' *previous learning* is matched to the current learning context. If a teacher is to give maximum opportunity for effective learning, then it is important to consider how to design learning so that all students are able to learn. The research literature suggests that an appropriate match of the students to the learning experience has a significant impact on their achievement (Bennett *et al.*, 1984).

A review by Tabberer (1996: 5) highlighted the importance of appropriate challenge in teaching:

> Research studies have added to the evidence that teachers too rarely provide children with tasks which are genuinely demanding and open ended. Teachers have been observed spending on average only 2 per cent of classroom time on questions regarded as offering challenge.

The task facing most teachers is how to find ways of managing the students' access to learning whilst maintaining the momentum of curriculum content. MacGilchrist *et al.* (1997: 36) suggest that there are four kinds of teaching design skills that effective teachers use that help them match and differentiate within their overall class plan. These are as follows:

- Effective teachers give feedback on pupil performance. They diagnose learning needs and note the progress being made. The monitoring, diagnosis, planning is part of an effective teacher's classroom repertoire and plays a vital role in learning design and implementation. In this respect, effective learning time is maximised when the teacher makes full use of all student feedback in order to plan appropriate learning activities.
- Effective teachers are skilled in the way they plan to group their students. They think through how they are going to spend their time to meet the needs of different groups. Student grouping has to be a deliberate part of learning design and can contribute to maximising effective learning time. The more effective the grouping the greater the potential for greater effective learning time.
- Effective teachers are able to design their teaching insofar as there are opportunities for students to practise and rehearse skills and

knowledge. The reinforcement and refinement of certain skills and behaviour is an important part of effective learning time. As highlighted in the later chapter on effective learning, repetition and reinforcement are two important components of effective learning.

- Effective teachers match the learning to the learners. Effective teachers build into the learning design quality extension activities for students to engage in if they finish a task before others in the class. Match is not just giving students work that is pitched to a level they can meet but designing work so that it extends students and builds upon students' learning.

Teachers have a range of teaching skills, styles, models and approaches that comprise a teaching repertoire. Some teachers have different sets of teaching skills or abilities from others. Consequently, to maximise the effectiveness of teachers requires presenting opportunities to extend and develop their individual teaching repertoires.

Within any school, teachers' expertise and practical competence will vary. In addition, different subject areas use quite diverse teaching approaches and instructional strategies. For many teachers the methods and approaches used in the classroom are repeated year on year primarily because they are effective. Opportunities to engage teachers in discussion about teaching methodology are important because they provide the basis for structured reflection. Yet, for optimum professional development to occur, strategies for reviewing and sharing teaching practices are of paramount importance and have been shown to promote professional growth. The next chapter considers how various approaches to professional development promote and enhance improvements in teaching.

QUESTIONS FOR FURTHER EXPLORATION

Improving schools place a particular emphasis upon enhancing the quality of teaching and learning. They recognise the importance of locating improvement efforts at both the school and classroom level.

(a) How far do your school-improvement efforts embrace the classroom level?
(b) Is your focus for school improvement directly linked to teaching and learning?
(c) How could you use the research findings concerning effective teaching and learning to assist in developmental work at the classroom level?

7 Improving teaching

Introduction

School improvement is ultimately about the enhancement of student progress, development and achievements, so it not surprising that most research evidence points towards the importance of teacher development in school development. It has been shown that schools that are successful facilitate the learning of both students and teachers. An essential component of successful school improvement interventions is the quality of professional development and learning. Collegial relations and collective learning are at the core of building the capacity for school improvement. This implies a particular form of teacher development that extends teaching repertoires and engages teachers in changing their practice (Hopkins *et al.*, 1997). Highly effective school improvement projects reflect a form of teacher development that concentrates upon enhancing teaching skills, knowledge and competency. It involves teachers in an exploration of different approaches to teaching and learning.

Whether informal or formal, continuous professional development is central to maintaining and enhancing the quality of teaching. Professional development tends to encompass different types of knowledge:

- research knowledge
- information from outside the school (for example from inspection)
- teachers' personal knowledge
- knowledge teachers construct as a group.

Over recent years, the Government has focused on teachers' professional development as part of the national framework of professional standards for teachers and as a way of maximising the impact of reforms. A study commissioned by the Teacher Training Agency examined professional development tracks for architects, doctors, engineers, nurses and solicitors and found that all the professions regarded the individual as being responsible for his or her own continuing professional development. This growing emphasis on professional development has resulted in increased funding of programmes to support national priorities, such as the literacy strategy, numeracy strategy and enhancing the ICT skills of teachers.

Despite such extensive and comprehensive programmes of professional development, the impact of such training upon classroom practice remains variable. There is evidence to show that many in-service training programmes fail to change teaching behaviours. As Joyce and Showers (1995: 13) note:

> Change in the classroom which involves more than extending the repertoire by acquiring new skills will mean changing attitudes, beliefs and personal theories and reconstructing a personal approach to teaching. INSET therefore needs to provide new experiences, support the anxieties which accompany not just the threat but the genuine difficulties of change and give people time to reflect, work things out and think things through.

The limitations of traditional in-service training within schools largely resides in the lack of ongoing support once the day is over. To improve this position implies changes to the way in which staff development is organised in most schools. In particular, this means establishing opportunities for immediate and sustained practice, classroom observation, collaboration and peer coaching.

REFLECTION

How is in-service training organised in your school?
How effective is it?
Is there evidence that it has changed teaching practices?

In most professional training for teachers there is a fundamental lack of connection between what Joyce (1992) terms 'the workshop' and 'the workplace'. In Joyce's (1992) view the workshop is the training-ground for developing new skills and knowledge – e.g. an INSET course or a professional qualification. Alternatively, the workplace is the classroom, department or school where new skills and knowledge will be utilised.

Skill acquisition and the ability to transfer 'workshop' knowledge to a range of situations necessitates 'on the job support'. It is difficult to transfer teaching skills from INSET sessions to classroom settings without alterations to the workplace conditions within the classroom, department and school. However, few schools have adapted the workplace to meet such staff development needs. In most schools the workroom and workplace remain separate and there is relatively little opportunity for follow-up support.

Teacher development for school improvement

All teachers have a set of developmental needs that relates to their age, experience, expertise and teaching context. A major consideration, therefore, in planning and encouraging staff development will be *how* it will contribute to individual and subject-area development. In the USA, a two-year study of professional development found that effective professional development could not be viewed as separate from the job of teaching (NFIE). This research concluded that effective professional development has to be focused upon classroom change and necessitates working with others.

To change classroom practice means a commitment among teachers to make explicit links between training and development. Joyce and Showers (1988: 30) have identified a number of key training components which when used in combination have much greater power than when they are used alone. The major components of effective staff development are:

* presentation of theory or description of skill or strategy;
* modelling or demonstration of skills or models of teaching;
* practice in simulated classroom settings;
* structured and open feedback (peer observation);
* coaching for application (Joyce and Showers, 1988: 34).

Based on this analysis it is clear that mutual observation and professional partnerships are key to improving the quality of teaching and learning. The establishment of critical friendships will increase professional learning and decrease feelings of isolation. By linking with one or more colleagues there is the possibility of mutual sharing of good practice. Learning with and from other teachers necessitates building professional trust and collaboration.

Collaboration

Improvements in teaching are most likely to occur where there are opportunities for teachers to work together and to learn from each other. Working with colleagues not only dispels feelings of professional isolation but assists in enhancing practice. Teachers are more able to implement new ideas within the context of supportive collaborative relationships or partnerships (Hargreaves, 1994). Collaboration among teachers strengthens resolve, permits vulnerabilities and carries people through the frustrations that accompany change in its early stages. It also eliminates the possibility of duplication and allows greater coordination and consistency of teaching approaches (Little, 1993).

By working collaboratively teachers are able to consider the different ways in which the subject-matter can be taught (Nias, 1989). Collaboration pools the collected knowledge, expertise and capacities of teachers within the subject area. It increases teachers' opportunities to learn from one another between classrooms, between subject areas and between schools (Darling-Hammond, 1990). The insulated and often segregated departments of secondary schools make it difficult for teachers to learn from one another. Consequently, schools need to build a climate of collaboration premised upon communication, sharing and opportunities for teachers to work together.

Collaboration improves the quality of student learning by improving the quality of teaching. It encourages risk-taking, greater diversity in teaching methods and an improved sense of efficacy among teachers. The principle of teacher collaboration is at the core of constructing a positive working community and is consistently listed in the effective schools literature as correlating positively with student outcomes (Mortimore *et al.*, 1994). Collaboration is important because it creates a collective professional confidence that allows teachers to interact more confidently and assertively.

Much more is now known about the conditions under which teachers develop to the benefit of themselves and their students. The problem remaining is how to build professional learning communities within schools, as these do not occur naturally. In many schools the norms of practice are not those of collaboration or mutual sharing but tend to be isolation or 'balkanisation'. If professional communities are to be established, then strategies for powerful change are required that integrate teacher development and school improvement.

For teacher development and school development to occur committing to certain kinds of collaboration is centrally important. However, collaboration without reflection and enquiry is little more than working collegially. For collaboration to influence professional growth and development it has to be premised upon mutual enquiry and sharing. There is sufficient evaluative evidence to show that when teachers are engaged in dialogue with each other about their practice then meaningful reflection and teacher learning occurs. As teachers search for new understanding or knowledge with other teachers the possibility and potential for school improvement is significantly increased. The school, as a learning community, is nurtured and sustained when individuals reflect upon, assess and discuss professional practice.

Reflection

Collaboration in dialogue and action can provide sources of feedback and comparison that prompt teachers to reflect on their own practice. Those teachers who recognise that enquiry and reflection are important processes in the classroom find it easier to sustain improvement effort around teaching and learning practices (Hopkins *et al.*, 1997). The reflective teacher is one who turns attention to the immediate reality of classroom practice. Reflection is centrally concerned with improving practice rather than collecting knowledge (Day, 1993). As each school, subject area and classroom are unique, reflective teachers develop their practice through engaging in enquiry and critical analysis of their teaching and the teaching of others.

There is now a growing literature that demonstrates and endorses the importance of evidence-based research as the basis for improving teaching. The analysis and application of research findings by teachers as part of their routine professional activity has been shown to have a positive effect upon the quality of teaching and learning (Harris and Hopkins, 1997; 1999). Lewis and Munn suggest that the overall aim of teacher research is to 'provide some systematic and reliable information that can be used as a basis for action' (1987: 6).

In order for teachers to be reflective about their practice there has to be 'a feedback loop', a means by which they can consider their work in a critical way. One powerful way in which teachers are encouraged to reflect upon and improve their practice is through a process of enquiry. It has been suggested that engaging in school-based enquiry is an essential element of the teacher's role. Enquiry and reflection are expected of teachers as part of their professional learning and development.

Engaging teachers in the process of 'systematic enquiry' does not necessarily mean a detailed knowledge of research but rather involvement in a form of systematic reflection on practice. MacBeath *et al.* argue that 'as in many other professions, the commitment to critical and systematic reflection on practice as a basis for individual and collective development is at the heart of what it means to be a professional teacher' (1988: 9).

The argument for research as a basis for teaching rests upon two main principles. Firstly, that teacher research is linked to the strengthening of *teacher judgement* and consequently to the self-directed improvement of practice. Secondly, that the most important focus for research is the curriculum in that it is the medium through which *the communication of knowledge* in schools takes place (Rudduck and Hopkins, 1995). As Stenhouse (1981: 16) noted

> it is not enough that teachers' work should be studied: they need to study it for themselves. What we need is a different view of research which begins with our own work and which is founded in curiosity and a desire to understand; which is stable, not fleeting, systematic in the sense of being sustained by a strategy.

Furthermore, Stenhouse (1979) argued for a change in what counts as research and the need to look for opportunities for teachers to engage in their own research and to communicate this to other practitioners.

Action enquiry

While there are many competing views about the process of action enquiry, it essentially encompasses *research* by teachers upon their own professional practice. Action enquiry draws upon the widest range of data collection methods and encompasses techniques from different research positions. Stenhouse (1981: 34) described it as 'Systematic and sustained enquiry, planned and self critical, which is subjected to public criticism and to empirical tests where these are appropriate'. Action enquiry is essentially practical and applied. It is driven by the need for teachers to solve practical, real-world problems. The research needs to be undertaken as part of teachers' practice rather than a bolt-on extra. Action research and enquiry is concerned with practical issues that arise naturally as part of professional activity. This practical orientation is one of the reasons why action enquiry remains a popular form of research activity among teachers. A major defining feature of action enquiry is its commitment to a cyclical process of research. Action enquiry is participatory in design as it involves the active participation of the researcher and those participating in the research.

Action enquiry is directly linked to the process of change. It provides a way forward for teachers to reflect upon practice and improve practice. There are many different approaches to action enquiry but the typical stages are as follows:

- identify a problem or concern;
- collect information;
- analyse information;
- decide about action;
- take action;
- evaluate impact of action.

The identification of a problem or issue should arise out of everyday teaching practice. Whatever the focus, the important dimension of action enquiry lies in investigating the question through collecting data. The data collection methods should relate directly to the problem or change and could include observation, interview, questionnaire, etc. The analysis should provide the basis for feedback on the issue or change, and provide the impetus for further action and subsequent enquiry.

The improvement of practice consists of realising the implicit values that lie within the practice itself. For teachers, values such as empowerment of learners and respect for students' views may be at the centre of their action-enquiry activities. Improving practice is about realising such values and necessarily involves a continuing process of reflection on the part of teachers. However, the kind of reflection encouraged by the action-enquiry process is quite distinctive from an ends-driven type of reasoning. The reflection is about choosing a course of action or a particular set of circumstances based upon a set of values or principles. Action enquiry improves practice by developing teachers' capacity to make judgements about their own practice. Implicit in this investigation is working with other teachers to improve classroom practice that inevitably involves classroom observation.

Classroom observation

Observation plays a crucial role, not only in classroom research but also more generally in supporting the professional growth of teachers (Day, 1999). It is a pivotal activity that links together reflection for the individual teacher and collaborative enquiry for pairs or groups of teachers. It also encourages the development of a language for talking about teaching and provides a means for working on developmental priorities for the staff as a whole (Southworth and Conner, 1999). Eraut (1994) has argued that as adult learners we need to be aware of our own and others' perceptions of our practice in order to develop fully as professionals. He suggests that the quality of skilled professional behaviour can be improved through:

- gaining feedback from independent observers;
- recording and reviewing our classroom behaviours;
- developing awareness of the impact of our actions;
- observing others in action;
- expanding our repertoire of routines.

Drummond *et al.* (1992: 42) describe observation as an essential and invaluable part of any educator's skills:

> Observation means more than watching and listening; it is a process by which educators can understand and give meaning

to what they see and hear, drawing on their own knowledge and experience.

Cooper (1989) noted that not only do we learn more about children and their learning by observing, we also learn more about the learning process and our involvement in it. Consequently, classroom or peer observation has to be at the heart of extending or developing teaching repertoires. It offers a prime source of professional feedback, necessary for improvement and the opportunity to engender and develop a language about teaching simply through talking to others about what happens in classrooms.

In setting up a classroom observation process there are a number of questions that need to be considered. Firstly, how will other teachers respond to the notion of classroom/peer observation? It is important that the purposes of the observation process are transparent from the outset and introduced to others as a means of professional development, rather than professional evaluation.

Secondly, the type of observational process that colleagues are encouraged to undertake needs some consideration. Hopkins (1993) usefully distinguishes between different methods of classroom observation: open, focused and structured. In an open observation, the observer simply notes what appears to him or her to be important or relevant. In an observation of this type ideas, issues or concerns are noted by the observer in an unstructured way. The limitation of this type of observation is the variability of the evidence base and the diversity of foci noted by the observer.

An alternative to this unstructured approach is a more focused approach where the foci for observation are predetermined and categories exist for recording information. This acts as a filter for the observation process and offers a clearer basis for feedback following the observation. Examples of using observation of this type could be to focus upon questioning techniques or the interaction of teachers and students. The result of collecting information of this type can be used for discussion with a view to improving teaching.

A third consideration when introducing classroom observation must be deciding the focus of the observation. If the purpose of the observation is to further professional learning and development then the observation must focus upon those teaching skills, approaches and models that are central to the teaching repertoire. It is essential, therefore, that a clear focus for the observation is both identified and agreed with colleagues. Teachers will need to encourage colleagues to focus upon some aspect of their teaching that they want to develop further. Only when observation is seen as developmental rather than judgmental has it any real chance of changing teaching behaviour.

Where observation fails it is often as a result of a lack of understanding about the purposes behind the process. Teachers need reassurance that the reasons for the observation are:

- sharing;
- development;
- support;
- enquiry.

Also, there need to be clear ground rules associated with the observation process. A set of questions establishing the ground rules appear in the box.

SETTING UP CLASSROOM OBSERVATION: KEY QUESTIONS

Have teachers been consulted about the process?
Is the process viewed as developmental?
Is there an agreed means of recording the observation?
Is there an agreed procedure for providing feedback?
Is confidentiality and trust assured?
Are there clear guidelines for observer and observed?

Classroom observation is an important form of professional development and can contribute directly to improvement in classroom practice. Hopkins (1993: 17) suggests 'that observation plays a crucial role, not only in classroom research but also more generally in supporting the professional growth of teachers . . . it seems to be the pivotal activity that links together reflection for the individual teacher and collaborative enquiry for groups of teachers.' Yet observation is a highly skilled activity that involves much more than just watching or listening. It involves recording and capturing critical moments in the teaching and learning interactions within classrooms. Observation is central to the teacher's understanding of the classroom and is therefore an essential component of school self-evaluation.

The particular approach to classroom observation adopted will depend upon the skills and experience of the observer. Hopkins (1993) distinguishes between four different methods of classroom observation: *open, structured, focused* and *systematic*. In structured and systematic observation an observation sheet or schedule will be used to record interactions. The data generated via classroom observation needs to be carefully analysed. Also, it is important that data are collected from a sequence of observations over time. In order to make judgements based on observational data it is important that other data are available to validate the findings.

Despite the well-established benefits of observation, there will be situations in which the opportunity to engage in observation will not be welcomed. Hence it is important to reinforce how those who engage in classroom observation can achieve breakthroughs in insight, action and effectiveness. Professional learning arises from building partnerships with other teachers and creating greater *interactive professionalism* among communities of teachers (Fullan and Hargreaves, 1992).

Improving teaching: improving schools

Schools that improve and continue to improve invest in the life of the school as a 'learning organisation' where members are constantly striving to seek new ways of improving their practice (Senge, 1990). An optimal school learning environment provides teachers with opportunities to work and learn together. It promotes sharing ideas and the open exchange of opinions and experiences. Teacher collaboration, reflection, enquiry and partnership are ways of building a professional development community. This is something that teachers can and should actively create themselves. Constructing and participating in the building of professional communities in schools is by its nature a vibrant form of teacher and school development.

Professional development is continuous learning focused upon the central goal of making a difference in the lives of diverse students. 'It is the sum total of formal and informal learning pursued and experienced by the teacher in a compelling learning environment under conditions of complexity and dynamic change' (Fullan 1993: 265). If the use of new practices is to be sustained and changes are to endure, regular opportunities for teachers to share perspectives and seek solutions will be required. Working collaboratively not only reduces the sense of isolation many teachers feel but also enhances the quality of the work produced. Working as part of a professional development community helps focus attention on shared purpose and the goals that lead to school improvement.

There are a number of important messages about the relationship between professional development and school improvement:

- It is important to foster deep collaboration and not superficial cooperation among the teaching staff.
- It is important to form partnerships within schools and to network with other schools and agencies.
- The capacity for school improvement is enhanced through teacher enquiry and action research.
- Schools need to allocate time for personal reflection and opportunities for teachers to talk together about teaching and learning.
- Developing the collective capability, expertise and commitment of teachers is one way of ensuring that all teachers contribute directly to school development and improvement.

If schools are serious about school improvement, the centrality of teacher development in that process needs to be recognised. For improvement to take place all stakeholders need to be involved and engaged. School improvement is at heart a collective activity where organisational learning is a dynamic and systemic process. As Wenger (1998: 262) notes, the focus is 'not on knowledge as an accumulated commodity but on learning as a social system productive of new meanings'. Schools that improve become learning communities that generate the capacity and capability to sustain that improvement. They are 'communities of practice' which provide a context for collaboration and the generation of shared meaning. 'Such communities hold the key to transformation – the kind that has real effects on people's lives' (Wenger, 1998: 85).

The next chapter synthesises the main themes emerging from this book and considers the central question of *how schools improve*. It highlights the main findings from the improvement research field and outlines key messages for schools. The chapter closes by reflecting upon 'what's in it for schools?'

QUESTIONS FOR FURTHER EXPLORATION

Schools that improve invest in teachers and their development. This chapter has highlighted four dimensions of teacher development:

Collaboration
Reflection
Observation
Enquiry

In your school:

(a) How prevalent are these four dimensions of professional development?
(b) How far are teachers encouraged to research their own practice?
(c) Is observation used for development purposes as well as for performance management?
(d) Is there evidence of collaboration between teachers?
(e) How could professional development be improved and enhanced?

8 School improvement: what's in it for schools?

Introduction

From this overview and synthesis of the school improvement field are some key messages for schools. There are a number of features that effective school improvement programmes share and these are worth underlining and reiterating. For school improvement to occur there must be the *will* to undertake change, the *skill* to make it happen and the *persistence* to see it through. School improvement is a way of generating organisational change and this inevitably requires both pressure and support.

For school improvement to be effective requires a high level of *commitment* amongst staff to innovation and change. Without this commitment it is clear that improvement efforts are unlikely to succeed. The support and involvement of staff is a critical component in securing meaningful change. An underlying feature of highly successful school improvement is the existence of *collaboration and mutual support* amongst staff. This will not occur unless efforts are made within the school to build the internal capacity and conditions that best foster and support school improvement.

It is also clear that successful school improvement focuses predominantly upon improving the quality of teaching and learning. To improve, schools need to locate their change efforts at the level of the classroom *and* the level of the school. Therefore, focusing on clearly identified student learning outcomes rather than broader organisational goals would seem to be the best way of securing improvement. This means ensuring that all school development is directly linked to specific issues of *teaching and learning* and that school and classroom development are mutually reinforcing.

The research findings show that schools have their own distinctive cultures and sometimes these work against organisational change. Hence the real target for school improvement is to change *school culture*. This involves building capacity within the school through an investment in teaching and teacher development. As Fullan (1991: 21) summarises, 'educational change depends on what teachers do and think, it's as simple and as complex as that'. Consequently, at the heart of school improvement is a focus upon *teacher development* and a desire to change school culture in order to promote change and development.

While school improvement does occur within a school, it is also important to recognise the part played by the wider community. *Partnerships* with parents, business and the local community are critically important in fostering school improvement. The involvement of those external to the school offers additional support but also provides a source of critical friendship. This 'external agency' has been shown to be an important factor in successful school improvement and a consistent element in those programmes and projects that work.

Essentially, school improvement is concerned with building professional learning communities. This means engaging teachers in a process of *enquiry and reflection*, in working with colleagues to problem-solve collectively and in working together as a learning organisation. In terms of organisational theory, if the school is a living system, it should seek to learn from within in order to develop and grow. School improvement requires teachers to work together to generate a better knowledge and understanding of the context in which they work. To develop the school as a learning organisation necessitates that all members contribute to knowledge creation and knowledge-building.

School improvement is *evolutionary and revolutionary*. It involves schools often in quite radical changes yet it is a process that evolves only over time. Without an adequate time-scale allowed for improvement efforts, the resulting change will be superficial and unsustainable. It has been estimated that to improve a school requires between three and four years. As Stoll and Myers (1998) rightly remind us, there are no quick fixes and those schools that seek such a panacea are likely to only become disillusioned and disappointed.

It is clear that school improvement cannot be externally mandated as schools can resist and undermine centrally driven change. If school improvement is to occur from within, it needs to focus upon its own developmental priorities rather than those that are externally imposed. There is, however, a tension between the amount of externally imposed reform and the time available for internal priorities. Many schools currently feel pressurised by the, often competing, demands of new government initiatives and strategies. This initiative overload in schools is, at worst, counter-productive to schools taking charge of their own change and development. It prevents many schools from concentrating on the issues and concerns of most importance in their school, in their particular context. It is unlikely that the constant stream of initiatives will subside in coming years; consequently the real challenge for schools is to harness the energy of external reform and use it for their own ends. The aligning of external change and internal priorities may not always be possible but it offers schools one way of reconciling the competing demands and tensions inherent in the current climate.

What messages for schools?

There are a number of important messages from the school improvement research field. These are as follows.

Be realistic but optimistic

The socio-economic contexts in which schools find themselves vary considerably. There are deep inequities in society and these are often reflected at the level of the individual school. While the school-effectiveness research has shown that *schools can make a difference*, it is important to recognise the potency of socio-economic factors in influencing student performance and achievement. This is not to advocate either pessimism or determinism but simply to highlight that schools located in areas of socio-economic deprivation with little parental support have a much tougher challenge in securing long-term, sustained school improvement.

Schools that face such challenges need to be realistic about the targets that are set for them or that they set themselves. While over-supporting schools may result in complacency, the pressure of unrealistic goals can prove equally counter-productive and result in failure or alienation. Exposing schools as 'failing' is unfortunately a strategy that is unlikely to encourage schools to invest in productive development and change. So being realistic does not mean lowering expectations but simply recognising the importance of context-specific improvement approaches (Harris and Chapman, 2002).

The school improvement literature confirms that schools even in the most challenging circumstances can improve and that there are school-improvement approaches that work. It is also evident that school improvement is not a remedial activity but is a means of developing all schools, even the most successful. Schools that are part of a school improvement programme or project will be more able to access new ideas and to share experience more readily. The networking component of school improvement is therefore important as it provides teachers with professional development opportunities and a way of linking with other teachers engaging in development work. Within the USA, there are a number of school improvement projects that are based on networks or loose coalitions. The evidence would suggest that schools benefit from working with other schools and are able to form learning systems where information and expertise are shared.

Engaging teachers and students

The success of school improvement depends upon the extent to which teachers and students are centrally engaged in the process of change. It is imperative that teachers play a leading role in directing and managing development, if it is to be successful. It is also important that students are engaged and involved in highlighting areas for change and development. Many schools have already recognised the importance of student participation and student voice in the process of school improvement. Students are best placed to suggest improvement, particularly at the classroom level. As Rudduck (2001: 15) suggests, listening to students assists schools in understanding the 'smaller picture' by eliciting their accounts and their views. It also contributes to restoring the link between teachers, students and learning.

By listening to the views of teachers and students about potential areas for change and development, the possibility for meaningful school improvement is enhanced. Engaging teachers in activities and processes that will allow them to implement and manage change is an important dimension of success. A particularly powerful way of generating school and classroom improvement occurs when teachers work together to generate and implement change. Where teachers and students have some ownership over the improvement agenda and where their views are actively sought the possibility of sustained school improvement increases.

Seek diversity not uniformity

It is apparent from the school improvement research that there is no one solution or approach to school improvement. Successful school improvement involves carefully selecting the developmental strategies that meet the particular needs of a school at a particular time. Schools go through various cycles of growth and development. Consequently it is important that the improvement strategies seek to 'fit' the developmental stage of the school.

The differences within schools tend to be larger than the differences between schools, therefore it is essential that schools seek strategies for improvement that address this range or variation. The need for differential strategies for improvement is particularly important at the departmental level where significant differences in performance can occur. While there may be a single or overarching school improvement strategy, there must be the opportunity for departments and subject areas to diversify their approaches to improvement and development.

Share and devolve leadership

Within improving schools leadership is not the single responsibility of an individual but a collective responsibility. Leadership is viewed in such schools in a distributed way where teachers are also leaders and contribute to the overall direction and vision of the school. The research evidence highlights the importance of 'professional leadership' in the pursuit of school improvement. Silns and Mulford (2002) have recently shown that the leadership characteristics of a school are important in enabling the school to operate as a learning organisation. Their work highlights the importance of the teacher leadership role and emphasises how distributed leadership enables others to act.

The more engaged teachers and students are in the school, the less there is need for the headteacher or senior management team to lead. The arguments against 'heroic leadership' are familiar and convincing. As Fullan (2001: 1) notes, 'superhuman leaders also do us another disservice: they are role models who can never be emulated by large numbers. Deep and sustained reform depends on many of us, not just the few who are destined to be extraordinary.' The evidence would suggest that if the source of leadership in the school is restricted to a few individuals, then organisational learning is severely constrained. The work of Silns and Mulford (2002: 31) highlights the importance of 'shared learning through teams of staff working together to augment the range of knowledge and skills available for the organisation to adapt to change and to anticipate future developments'. A school that operates with limited opportunities for leadership will be a school that places a self-imposed limit upon its ability to improve. As Fullan (2001: 137) suggests, 'leadership in a culture of change will be judged as effective or ineffective not by who you are as a leader but by what leadership you produce in others'. This implies that those within a school form a community of leaders and that leadership is concerned with sharing rather than retaining power.

Build and nurture community

In order to improve and to sustain improvement over time schools need to build and nurture a sense of professional community. In the most effective schools, there is evidence of positive relationships both within and outside the school. Barth (1990: 45) describes a professional community as 'one where adults and students learn and each energizes and contributes to the learning of the other'. A professional community is one in which there are shared norms and values among teachers and students. These norms and values represent the fundamental beliefs of those within the community and become the defining purpose of the school. To build a professional community requires schools to consider the type of school culture that prevails and to seek ways of changing it for the better.

Learning within an organisation is optimal in an environment of shared leadership and shared power. To foster such an environment requires team work, collaboration and a commitment to enquiry.

Connections are particularly important in building community. As Sergiovanni (2001: 63) notes, 'community is something most of us want in order to experience the sense and meaning that we need in our lives. We cannot go it alone. We have to be connected somehow, somewhere. Community is a particularly important source of connection for children and young people.' If the needs of students to belong are not met by the school then they will find belonging outside the school.

In schools that are improving there are shared norms, shared values, agreed goals and common aspirations. These are schools where the social relations are functional and where trust and respect are at the core of all developmental work. This does not occur by chance but results from the deliberate effort of staff and students to communicate and to collaborate with one another. Sergiovanni (2001) notes that such 'communities of responsibility' are far from easy to cultivate but are necessary to generate and sustain school improvement over time.

What's in it for schools?

So, what's in it for schools? Why pursue school improvement? At one level school improvement is a way of schools achieving organisational development and growth. At another level school improvement has a moral purpose and is intrinsically linked to the life-chances and achievements of all students. So the real question becomes, *what's in it for those who engage in school improvement?*

School improvement is essentially about building communities and establishing positive relationships within those communities. It has at its core the fundamental belief that schools can and do make a difference and that this difference can be significantly enhanced. Rutter *et al.* (1979: 13) provide one of the most hopeful statements about school improvement by highlighting that the factors that influence school performance are 'open to modification by staff rather than fixed by external constraints'. In other words, schools can improve, schools can change and school performance is not a fixed or predetermined entity.

Evidence would suggest that those schools engaged in improvement activities build communities that are collaborative and empowering. They foster positive relationships and allow all voices to be heard and acknowledged. In this sense, school improvement means moving from a culture of individualism to what Clarke (2000: 7) calls 'a renewed sense of social responsibility'. So, what's in it for schools? At its most profound, it is about making a difference to the lives of young people and at its most pragmatic it is about knowing *how* to do this most effectively.

The stated intention of this book was to assist schools in understanding *how* school improvement takes place. It is clear that schools that invest in the development of their teachers also invest in the development of the school. When teachers are given power to act and are involved in the development of the school there is more potential for school growth. In a climate of collegiality rather than congeniality teachers are more likely to trust one another and to encourage innovation and change (Barth, 1990).

Schools are capable of improving themselves if the conditions are right and the relationships within the school are supportive of change. It will inevitably be more difficult to create the optimum internal conditions in the face of relentless external change. Schools are currently caught between the demands of policy-makers and the needs of the students and parents in their community. Fullan (1999) argues that schools are inevitably pulled in two directions, by stable and less stable forces, and that 'the dynamics of the successful organisation are of irregular cycles and discontinuous trends' (Fullan, 1999: 4). Consequently, by building strong professional communities schools will be more able to swim with the tide of external reform and will be more adept at coping with the pressures of external change.

Barth (1990: 158) describes a school as 'four walls surrounding a future'. This image captures the potency and possibility of school improvement. It reminds us that school improvement is much more than raising test scores or increasing grades. Its essence lies in building school communities that are collaborative, inclusive and ultimately empowering. For it is only within such communities that the potential of both students and teachers will be fully realised. It is this aspiration that lies at the heart of school improvement and ensures that schools remain places where, above all, learning matters.

QUESTIONS FOR FURTHER EXPLORATION

Schools that build professional learning communities are most likely to improve and to sustain improvement. By fostering collaboration and trust between staff and students, schools are more able to generate the change and development necessary for improvement.

(a)   How far is your school a learning community?

(b)   How much trust, collaboration and cooperation is in evidence on a daily basis?

(c)   What steps can be taken to ensure that your school becomes or remains a learning community – in the short, medium and long term?

(d)   How do you currently contribute to this community?

References

Ainscow, M., Hopkins, D., Southworth, G. and West, M. (1994) *Creating the Conditions for School Improvement*. London: David Fulton.

Barth, R. (1990) *Improving Schools from Within: Teachers, Parents and Principals Can Make a Difference*. San Francisco: Jossey-Bass.

Bennett, N. (1984) *Teaching Styles and Pupil Progress*. London: Sage.

Bennett, N., and Harris, A. (2000) 'Hearing truth from power', *School Effectiveness and School Improvement. An International Journal of Research Policy and Practice*, 5 (4), pp. 533–50.

Bennett, N. and Harris, A. (2001) 'School effectiveness and school improvement: future challenges and possibilities', in Harris, A. and Bennett, N.(eds), *School Effectiveness and School Improvement Alternative Perspectives*. London: Cassell.

Bennis, W.E., Benne, K. and Chin, R. (1969) *The Planning of Change*. London: Holt, Rineholt and Winston.

Beresford, J. (1998) *Collecting Information for School Improvement*. London: David Fulton.

Beresford, J. (2000) 'Student conditions and school improvement' (unpublished PhD thesis) University of Nottingham.

Bhindi, N. and Duignan, P. (1996) 'Leadership 2020: a visionary paradigm', paper presented at Commonwealth Council for Educational Administration International Conference, Kuala Lumpur.

Blase, J. and Anderson, G. (1995) *The Micro-Politics of Educational Leadership: From Control to Empowerment*. London: Cassell.

Busher, H. and Harris, A. (2000) *Leading Subject: Areas Improving Schools*. London: Paul Chapman.

Caldwell, B.J. and Spinks, J.M. (1998) *Beyond the Self-Managing School*. London: Falmer Press.

Chapman, C. (2000) 'OFSTED and classroom improvement' (unpublished paper) University of Nottingham.

Clarke, P. (2000) *Learning Schools, Learning Systems.* London: Continuum Press.

Comer, J. (1988) 'Educating poor minority children', *Scientific American*, November, pp. 42–8.

Cooper, H. (1989) 'Does reducing student to instructor ratios affect achievement?', *Educational Psychologist*, 24, pp. 78–98.

Creemers, B.P.M. (1994), *The Effective Classroom.* London: Cassell.

Dalin, P. (1996) *School Culture.* London: Cassell.

Dalin, P. (1998) *School Development: Theories and Strategies.* London: Cassell.

Dalin, P., with Rolff, H.-G. and Kleekamp, B. (1993) *Changing the School Culture.* London: Cassell.

Dalin, P. and Rust, V.D. (1996) *Towards Schooling for the Twenty First Century.* London: Cassell.

Darling-Hammond, L. (1990) 'Teacher Professionalism: Why and How?' in A. Lieberman, (ed.), *Schools as Collaborative Cultures: Creating the Future Now.* London: Falmer Press.

Day, C. (1993) 'Reflection: a necessary but not sufficient condition for professional development', *British Educational Research Journal*, 19 (1), pp. 83–93.

Day, C. (1999) *Developing Teachers: The Challenges of Lifelong Learning.* London: Falmer Press.

Day, C., Hall, C. and Whitaker, P. (1998) *Developing Leadership in Primary Schools.* London: Paul Chapman.

Day, C., Harris, A. and Hadfield, M. (2000) 'Grounding knowledge of schools in stakeholder realities: a multi-perspective study of effective school leaders', *School Leadership and Management.*

Day, C., Harris, A., Hadfield, M., Tolley, H. and Beresford, J. (2000) *Leading Schools in Times of Change.* Milton Keynes: Open University Press.

Deal, T.E. and Peterson, K.D. (1994) *The Leadership Paradox: Balancing Logic and Artistry in Schools.* San Francisco: Jossey-Bass

DES (1977) *Ten Good Schools.* London: Department of Education and Science.

Drummond, M.J., Rouse, D. and Pugh, G. (1992) *Making Assessment Work.* Nottingham: NES Arnold and the National Children's Bureau.

Duignan, P.A. and Macpherson, R.J.S. (1992) *Educative Leadership: A Practical Theory for New Administrators and Managers.* London: Falmer Press.

Dweck, C. and Repucci, N. (1973) 'Learned helplessness and reinforcement responsibility in children', *Journal of Personality and Social Psychology*, 31 (4).

Earl, L. and Lee, L. (1998). *Evaluation of the Manitoba School Improvement Programme.* Winnipeg: Manitoba School Improvement Programme.

Elmore, R. (1995) 'Structural reform in educational practice', *Educational Researcher*, 24 (9), December, pp. 23–6.

Eraut, M. (1994) *Developing Professional Knowledge and Competence*. London: Falmer Press.

Fullan, M. (1991) *The New Meaning of Educational Change*. London: Cassell.

Fullan, M. (1992) *Successful School Improvement*. Buckingham: Open University Press.

Fullan, M. (1993) *Change Forces: Probing the Depths of Educational Reform*. London: Falmer Press.

Fullan, M. (1999) *Change Forces: The Sequel*. Buckingham: Open University Press.

Fullan, M. (2001) *Leading in a Culture of Change*. San Francisco: Jossey-Bass.

Fullan, M. and Hargreaves, A. (1992) *What's Worth Fighting For: Working Together for Your School*. Buckingam: Open University Press.

Glickman, C. (1990) 'Pushing school reforms to a new edge: the seven ironies of school empowerment', *Phi Delta Kappan*, pp. 68–75.

Glickman, C.D. (1993) *Renewing America's Schools: A Guide for School-Based Action*. San Francisco: Jossey-Bass.

Gray, J. and Wilcox, B. (1995) *Good School, Bad School: Evaluating Performance and Encouraging Improvement*. Buckingham: Open University Press.

Gray, J., Hopkins, D. and Reynolds, D. (1999) *Improving Schools: Performance and Potential*. Milton Keynes: Open University Press.

Gronn, P. (2000) 'Distributed properties: a new architecture for leadership', *Educational Management and Administration*, 28 (3), pp. 317–38.

Hallinger, P. and Heck, R. (1996) 'Reassessing the principal's role in school effectiveness: a critical review of empirical research 1980–1995', *Educational Administration Quarterly*, 32 (1), pp. 4–5.

Hargreaves, A. (1994) *Changing Teachers: Changing Times*. London: Cassell.

Hargreaves, A. and Hopkins, D. (1994) *School Development Planning*. London: Cassell.

Hargreaves, A., Lieberman, A., Fullan, M., and Hopkins, D. (eds) (1998) *The International Handbook of Educational Change* (4 vols). Dordrecht, Netherlands: Kluwer Academic Publishers.

Harris, A. (1998) 'Improving the effective department: strategies for growth and development', *Education Management and Administration*, 26 (3), pp. 269–78.

Harris, A. (1999a) *Teaching and Learning in the Effective School*. London: Arena Press.

Harris, A. (1999b) *Effective Subject Leadership: A Handbook of Staff Development Activities*. London: David Fulton Press.

Harris, A. (2000a) 'Successful school improvement in the United Kingdom and Canada', *Canadian Journal of Education, Administration and Policy*, 15, pp. 1–8.

Harris, A. (2000b) 'Effective leadership and departmental improvement', *Westminster Studies in Education*, 23, pp. 81–90.

Harris, A. (2000c) 'What works in school improvement? Lessons from the field and future directions', *Educational Research*, 42 (1), pp. 1–11.

Harris, A. (2001a) 'Building the capacity for school improvement', *School Leadership and Management*, 21 (3), pp. 261–70.

Harris, A. (2001b) 'Department improvement and school improvement: a missing link?' *British Educational Research Journal*, 27 (4), pp. 477–87.

Harris, A. and Bennett, N. (eds) (2001) *School Effectiveness and School Improvement: Alternative Perspectives*. London: Cassell.

Harris, A. and Chapman, C. (2002) 'Democratic leadership for school improvement in challenging contexts', a paper presented at the International Congress on School Effectiveness and Improvement, Copenhagen.

Harris, A. and Hopkins, D. (1999) 'Teaching and Learning and the Challenge of Educational Reform', *School Effectiveness and School Improvement. An International Journal of Research Policy and Practice*, 10(1), pp. 257–67.

Harris, A. and Hopkins, D. (2000) 'Alternative Perspectives on School Improvement', *School Leadership and Management*, 20 (1), pp. 9–15.

Harris, A. and Young, J. (2000) 'Comparing school improvement programmes in the United Kingdom and Canada: lessons learned', *School Leadership and Management*. 20 (1), pp. 31–43.

Harris, A., Day, C. and Hadfield, M. (2001) 'Headteachers' views of effective school leadership', *International Studies in Educational Administration*, 29 (1), pp. 29–39.

Harris, A., Jamieson, I.M. and Russ, J. (1996) *School Improvement and School Effectiveness: A Practical Guide*. London: Pitman Press.

Harris, A., Preedy, M. and Bennett, N. (eds) (1997) *Organisational Effectiveness and Improvement*. Milton Keynes: Open University Press.

Hopkins, D. (1987) *Improving the Quality of Schooling*. Lewes: Falmer Press.

Hopkins, D. (1990) 'The International School Improvement Project (ISIP) and effective schooling: towards a synthesis', *School Organisation*, 10 (3), pp. 129–94.

Hopkins, D. (1993) *A Teacher's Guide to Classroom Research*. London: Falmer Press.

Hopkins, D. (1995) *School Based Evaluation*. London: Falmer Press.

Hopkins, D. (1996) 'Towards a theory for school improvement', in J. Gray, D. Reynolds, C. Fitz-Gibbon (eds) *Merging Traditions: The Future of Research on School Effectiveness and School Improvement*. London: Cassell.

Hopkins, D. (2000) 'Powerful learning powerful teaching powerful', *Journal of Educational Change*, 1(2), pp. 135–54.

Hopkins, D. (2001) *School Improvement for Real*. London: Falmer Press.

Hopkins, D. and Harris, A. (1997). 'Improving the Quality of Education for All', *Support for Learning*, 12 (4), pp. 147–51.

Hopkins, D. and Harris, A. (2000) 'Differential strategies for school development' in D.Van Veen and C. Day (eds) *Professional Development and School Improvement: Strategies for Growth*. Mahwah, NJ: Erlbaum.

Hopkins, D. and Levin, B. (2000) 'Government policy and school development', *School Leadership and Management*. 20 (1), pp. 15–30.

Hopkins, D. and West, M. (1994) 'Teacher development and school improvement', in D. Walling (ed.) *Teachers as Learners*. Bloomington, IN: PDK.

Hopkins, D., Ainscow, M. and West, M. (1994). *School Improvement in an Era of Change*. London: Cassell.

Hopkins, D., Ainscow, M. and West, M. (1996) 'Unravelling the complexities of school improvement: a case study of the Improving the Quality of Education for All' in A. Harris, M. Preedy and N. Bennett (eds) (1997) *Organisational Effectiveness and Improvement*. Milton Keynes: Open University Press.

Hopkins, D., Harris, A. and Jackson, D. (1997) 'Understanding the school's capacity for development: growth states and strategies', *School Leadership and Management*.17 (3), pp. 401–11.

Hopkins, D., West, M. and Ainscow, M. (1996) *Improving the Quality of Education for All*. London: David Fulton Publishers.

Hopkins, D., Harris, A., Singleton, C. and Watts, R. (2000) *Creating the Conditions for Teaching and Learning*. London: David Fulton Press.

Hopkins, D., Harris, A., West, M., Ainscow, M. and Beresford, J. (1997) *Creating the Conditions for Classroom Improvement*. London: David Fulton Publishers.

Huberman, M. and Miles, M. (1984) *Innovation Up Close*. New York: Plenum Press.

Jackson, D. (2000) 'The school improvement journey: perspectives on leadership', *School Leadership and Management*, 20 (1), pp. 61–79.

Joyce, B. (1988) *Student Achievement through Staff Development*. London: Longman.

Joyce, B. (ed.) (1990) *Changing School Culture through Staff Development*. Alexandra: Association for Supervision and Curriculum Development.

Joyce, B. (1992) 'Cooperative learning and staff development: teaching the method with the method', *Cooperative Learning*, 12 (2), pp. 10–13.

Joyce, B. and Showers, B. (1988) *Information Processing: Models of Teaching*. Aptos: CA Booksend Laboratories.

Joyce, B. and Showers, B. (1995) *Student Achievement through Staff Development*. White Plains, NY: Longman.

Joyce, B. and Weil, M. (1996) *Models of Teaching* (4th edition). Englewood Cliffs, NJ: Prentice-Hall.

Joyce, B., Calhoun, E. and Hopkins, D. (1997) *Models of Learning: Tools for Teaching*. Buckingham: Open University Press.

Joyce, B., Calhoun, E., and Hopkins, D. (1999) *The New Structure of School Improvement: Inquiring Schools and Achieving Students*. Buckingham: Open University Press.

Kyriacou, C. (1986) *Effective Teaching in Schools*. Oxford: Basil Blackwell.

Kyriacou, C. (1991) *Essential Teaching Skills*. Oxford: Basil Blackwell.

Lambert, L. (1998) *Building Leadership Capacity in Schools*. Alexandria, VA: Association for Supervision and Curriculum Development.

Leithwood, K. and Louis, K.S. (2000) *Organisational Learning in Schools*. Netherlands: Swets and Zeitlinger.

Leithwood, K. and Jantzi, D. (1990). 'Transformational leadership: how principals can help reform school cultures', *School Effectiveness and School Improvement*, 1 (4), pp. 249–80.

Leithwood, K. and Jantzi, D. (2000) 'The effects of transformational leadership on organisational conditions and student engagement', *Journal of Educational Administration* 38 (2), pp. 112–29.

Leithwood, K., Jantzi, D. and Steinback, R. (1999) *Changing Leadership for Changing Times*. Buckingham: Open University Press.

Levine, D. and Lezotte, L. (1990). *Unusually Effective Schools: A Review of Research and Practice*. Madison, WI: National Centre for Effective Schools Research and Development.

Lewin, K. (1947) 'Group divisions and social change', in T.M. Newcomb and E.L. Hartley (eds) *Readings in Social Psychology*, New York: Henry Holt.

Lewin, K. (1948) *Resolving Social Conflicts*. New York: Harper and Row.

Lewis, I. and Munn, P. (1987) 'So you want to do research! A guide for teachers on how to formulate research questions', *Scottish Council for Research in Education* (SCRE) Practitioner Mini-paper 2.

Little, J.W. (1993) 'Teachers' professional development in a climate of educational reform', *Educational Evaluation and Policy Analysis*, 15 (2), pp. 129–51.

Louis, K.S., Marks, H. and Kruse, S. (1996) 'Teachers' professional community in re-structuring schools', *American Research Journal*, 33 (4), pp. 757–98.

MacBeath, J. (ed.) (1988) *Effective School Leadership: Responding to Change*. London: Paul Chapman.

MacGilchrist, B., Myers, K. and Reed, J. (1997) *The Intelligent School*. London: Paul Chapman.

Miles, M., Elkholm, M. and Vandenberghe, R. (eds) (1987) *Lasting School Improvement: Exploring the Process of Institutionalisation*. Leuven, Belgium: ACCO.

Miles, M.B., Louis, K.S., Rosenblum, S., Ciploone, A. and Farrar, E. (1988) *Improving the Urban High School: A Preliminary Report*. Boston: Center for Survey Research, University of Massachusetts.

Mitchell, C. and Sackney, L. (2000) *Profound Improvement: Building Capacity for a Learning Community*. Lisse: Swets and Zeitlinger.

Morgan, G. (1997) *Images of Organisation*. London: Sage.

Morley, L. and Rassol, N. (1999) *School Effectiveness: Fracturing the Discourse*. London: Falmer Press.

Mortimore, P. (2000) *The Road to School Improvement*. Lisse: Swets and Zeitlinger.

Mortimore, P., Sammons, P. and Thomas, S. (1994) 'School effectiveness and value added measures', *Assessment in Education: Principles, Policy and Practice*, 1 (3), pp. 315–32.

Muijs, D. and Reynolds, D. (2001) *Effective Teaching: Evidence and Practice*. London: Paul Chapman.

Murphy, J. and Louis, K. (eds) *Handbook of Research on Educational Administration*. San Francisco, CA: Jossey-Bass.

Myers, K. (1995) 'Intensive care for the chronically sick', paper presented at the European conference on educational research, Bath.

Myers, K. (1996) *Schools Make a Difference*. London: Falmer Press.

Nias, J. (1989). *Primary Teachers Talking*. London: Routledge and Kegan Paul.

Ouston, J. (1998) 'Introduction', *School Leadership and Management*, 18, pp. 317–20.

Ouston, J. (1999) 'School effectiveness and school improvement: critique of a movement', in Bush *et al.* (eds) *Educational Management: Redefining Theory, Policy and Practice*. London: Paul Chapman.

Patterson, M.G., West, M.A., Lawthom, R. and Nickell, S. (1997) *Impact of People Management Practices on Business Performance*. London: Institute of Personnel and Development.

Reynolds, D., Sammons, P., Stoll, L., Barber, M., and Hillman, J. (1996) 'School Effectiveness and School Improvement in the United Kingdom', *School Effectiveness and School Improvement*, 7 (2), pp. 133–58.

Reynolds, D., Creemers, B.P.M., Nesselrodt, P.S., Schaffer, E.C., Stringfield, S. and Teddlie, C. (1994) *Advances in School Effectiveness Research and Practice*. Place: Elsevier Science.

Riley (2000) *Whose School is it Anyway?* London: Falmer Press.

Rosener, J.B. (1990) 'Ways Women Lead', *Harvard Business Review*. November/December.

Rosenholtz, S. (1989) *Teachers Workplace*. New York: Longman.

Rosenshine, B. (1983) 'Teaching functions in instructional programs', *The Elementary School Journal*. 83 (4), pp. 335–51.

Rudduck, J. (2001) 'Students and school improvement: transcending the cramped conditions of time', *Improving Schools*, 4 (2), pp. 7–15.

Rudduck, J. and Hopkins, D. (1995) 'Introduction', in J. Rudduck, and D. Hopkins (eds) *Research as a Basis for Teaching: Readings from the Work of Lawrence Stenhouse*. London: Falmer Press.

Rudduck, J., Chaplain, R. and Wallace, G. (1996) *School Improvement: What Pupils Can Tell Us?* London: David Fulton Press.

Rutter, M., Maughan, B., Mortimore, P., and Ouston, J. (1979) *Fifteen Thousand Hours.* London: Open Books.

Sackney, L., Walker, K. and Hajal, V. (1998) 'Principal and teacher perspectives on school improvement', *Journal of Educational Management,* 1 (1) pp. 45–63.

Sammons, P. (2000) *School Effectiveness: Coming of Age.* Lisse: Swets and Zeitlinger.

Sammons, P., Thomas, S. and Mortimore, P. (1997) *Forging Links: Effective Schools and Effective Departments.* London: Paul Chapman.

Sarason, S. (1990) *The Predictable Failure of Educational Reform.* San Francisco: Jossey-Bass.

Scheerens, J. (1992) *Effective Schooling: Research, Theory and Practice.* London: Cassell.

Schein, E. (1992) *Organisational Culture and Leadership* (2nd edn). San Francisco, CA: Jossey-Bass.

Senge, P. (1990) *The Fifth Discipline: The Art and Practice of the Learning Organisation.* New York: Doubleday.

Sergiovanni, T.J. (1998) 'Leadership as pedagogy, capital development and school effectiveness', *International Journal of Leadership in Education,* 1 (1), pp. 37–46.

Sergiovanni, T. (2000) *The Lifeworld of Leadership.* London: Jossey-Bass.

Sergiovanni, T. (2001) *Leadership: What's in it for Schools?* London: Routledge-Falmer.

Shakeshaft, C. (1996) *Women in Educational Administration.* Newbury Park: Unwin.

Silns, H. and Mulford, B. (2002) 'Leadership and school results', *Second International Handbook of Educational Leadership and Administration* (in press).

Sizer, T. (1992) *Horace's School.* New York: Houghton Mifflin.

Sizer, T.R. (1989) 'Diverse practice, shared ideals: the essential school' in H. Walberg, and J. Lane (eds) *Organising for Learning: Towards the 21st Century.* Reston, VA: NASSP.

Slavin, R. (1996) *Education for All.* Lisse, Netherlands: Swets and Zeitlinger.

Slavin, R., Madden, N.A., Dolan, L.J., and Wasik, B.A. (1996) *Every Child, Every School: Success for All.* Thousand Oaks, CA: Corwin Press.

Slavin, R., Madden, N.A., Karweit, N.L., Dolan, L., Wasik, B.A., Ross, S.M. and Smith, L. J. (1994) "Whenever and Wherever we Choose': The Replication of 'Success for All", *Phi Delta Kappan,* April, pp. 639–47.

Slee, R., Weiner, G. and Tomlinson, S. (eds) (1988) *School Effectiveness for Whom? Challenges to the School Effectiveness and School Improvement Movements.* London: Falmer Press.

Southworth, G. (1995) *Talking Heads: Voices of Experience.* Cambridge: University of Cambridge Institute of Education.

Southworth, G. and Conner, C. (1999) *Managing Improving Primary Schools*. London: Falmer Press.

Stenhouse, L. (1979) 'Research as a basis for teaching', in J. Ruddick and D. Hopkins (eds) (1995) *Research as a Basis for Teaching: Readings from the Work of Lawrence Stenhouse*. London: Falmer Press.

Stenhouse, L. (1981) 'Action Research and the Teacher's Responsibility for the Educational Process', in J. Ruddick and D. Hopkins (eds) (1995) *Research as a Basis for Teaching Readings from the Work of Lawrence Stenhouse*. London: Falmer Press.

Stoll, L. (1999) 'Building capacity for improvement' (unpublished paper).

Stoll, L. and Fink, D. (1996). *Changing our Schools: Linking School Effectiveness and School Improvement*. Buckingham: Open University Press.

Stoll, L. and Myers, K. (1998) *No Quick Fixes: Perspectives on Schools in Difficulty*. London: Falmer Press.

Stoll, L., Wikeley, F. and Reezight, G. (2000) 'Developing a common model? comparing effective school improvement across European countries', paper presented at 13th meeting of the International Congress on School Effectiveness and Improvement, Hong Kong.

Stringfield, S. (1995) 'Attempting to enhance students' learning through innovative programs: the case for schools evolving into high reliability organizations', *School Effectiveness and School Improvement*, 6 (1), pp. 67–96.

Stringfield, S., Reynolds, D. and Schaffer, E. (2001) 'The High Reliability Project: some preliminary results and analyses', paper presented at 14th meeting of the International Congress on School Effectiveness and Improvement, Toronto, Canada.

Tabberer, R. (1996) *Effective Teaching: A Review of Literature*. Slough: NFER.

Teddlie, C. and Reynolds, D. (2000) *The International Handbook of School Effectiveness Research*. London: Falmer Press.

Thrupp, M. (1999) *Schools Improvement: Let's Be Realistic*. London: Falmer Press.

Van Velzen, W., Miles, M., Elholm, M., Hameyer, U. and Robin, D. (1985) *Making School Improvement Work*. Leuven, Belgium: ACCO.

Walker, K., Shakotko, D. and Pullman, E. (1998) 'Towards a further understanding of trust and trustworthiness', paper presented to the Values and Educational Leadership Conference, University of Toronto, Ontario.

Wenger, E. (1998) *Communities of Practice: Learning, Meaning and Identity*. Cambridge: Cambridge University Press.

West, M., Jackson, D., Harris, A. and Hopkins, D. (eds) (2000) 'Leadership for school improvement', in K. Riley and K. Seashore Louis, *Leadership for Change*. London: RoutledgeFalmer.

Wood, D. (1988) *How Children Think and Learn*. London: Blackwell Publishers.

Index